Praise for *Deliberate Creative Teams*

"When I wanted to equip my marketing team with tools to help them grow their creative thinking to greater heights, I called Dr. Amy Climer. Her book delivers research-based strategies and tangible methods that are difference-makers for teams. I recommend it for all leaders seeking innovation."

ROBERT GOTTLIEB, president of marketing, Fox Sports

"In *Deliberate Creative Teams*, Dr. Amy Climer beautifully encapsulates the essentials of fostering innovation. This book is stuffed with wisdom and propelled by relatable stories, practical exercises, and solid evidence."

LIANE DAVEY, PhD, bestselling author of *You First* and *The Good Fight*

"Dr. Amy Climer has written a wonderful book! She shows you how to be deliberate with your creativity. You'll learn a set of everyday practices that lead to consistent, successful creativity—for both you and your team."

KEITH SAWYER, professor, creativity researcher, and bestselling author of *Zig Zag* and *Group Genius*

"As someone who's spent years helping leaders build powerful, resilient teams, I know that true creativity isn't a gift—it's a skill you can teach and a culture you can foster. *Deliberate Creative Teams* is a powerful hands-on guide that demystifies creativity in a way that every team can understand and apply. This isn't about one-off brainstorming; it's a road map for consistently nurturing innovation and tapping into each team member's potential. Dr. Amy Climer combines her expertise and personal experience to show leaders exactly how to build an environment where creativity and collaboration drive results that matter. If you want your team to solve problems and transform challenges into breakthrough moments, this is the book to read."

ANTON J. GUNN, CEO, 937 Strategy Group

"Dr. Amy Climer's *Deliberate Creative Teams* is an inspiring, practical guide for building creativity and innovation within teams. Packed with stories, research, and tools, this book is a valuable addition to any leader's tool kit!"

JEAN ANDERSON, librarian and consulting services coordinator, South Central Library System

"*Deliberate Creative Teams* is a must-read for managers, leaders, and anyone working with teams who wants to foster creative collaboration and connection. The Deliberate Creative Team system is a clear, powerful framework that provides the tools and strategies leaders need to help their teams thrive. Dr. Amy Climer presents relatable examples and actionable strategies for anyone looking to lead innovative teams. This book will absolutely find a place on my shelf of go-to creativity resources!"

DR. AMY WHITNEY, director of Center for Innovation, University of North Dakota

"*Deliberate Creative Teams* is a game-changer for anyone working on a team, with its practical tools and insightful strategies to foster true collaboration and innovation. Dr. Amy Climer seamlessly blends theory and practice, equipping readers with a system to not only be more creative but become better teammates and leaders. The concepts of cooperative versus collaborative teams and relational versus task conflict have already shifted how I approach my work, and Dr. Climer's real-world examples bring the lessons to life. This book will inspire you to rethink how your team operates and help you push for meaningful change."

DR. NICK ORLOWSKI, director of school leadership, CS Partners

"Informed by real-world experience and cutting-edge research, Dr. Amy Climer delivers a powerful and easy-to-use handbook on team effectiveness."

GERARD J. PUCCIO, PhD, distinguished professor and chair, Center for Applied Imagination, SUNY Buffalo State College

DELIBERATE
CREATIVE
TEAMS

HOW TO LEAD FOR
INNOVATIVE RESULTS

Amy Climer, PhD

DELIBERATE
CREATIVE
TEAMS

PAGE TWO

Cataloguing in publication information is
available from Library and Archives Canada.
ISBN 978-1-77458-493-4 (paperback)
ISBN 978-1-77458-494-1 (ebook)

Page Two
pagetwo.com

Edited by Kendra Ward
Copyedited by David Marsh
Cover design, interior design, and graphics by Taysia Louie
Climer® Card illustrations by Amy Climer, PhD

climerconsulting.com

For all the leaders who are using
creativity to do good in the world.

For my dad, who passed along
his propensity for ideas.

For my mom, who passed along
her ability to get things done.

For Julie, who is the best wife ever.

Contents

You're Not Creative
(or So You Were Told)

I N MY FIRST year of college I eagerly signed up for a class called Studio Art for Non-Majors. I was a biology major, but the course satisfied one of the general education requirements. On the first day of class the professor said, "If you don't have artistic talent, you are not going to do well in this class." I remember thinking, "Wait a minute. Isn't this class for people *not* majoring in art? Jerk." My next thought was "Well, what the heck. I've made lots of art and have some talent. I'll stick it out and see what happens."

What happened was I worked really hard and barely got a B. In high school I was mostly an A student, so I was not proud of this B.

I learned a lot in that class, but not much about art.

For sixteen weeks, I watched the teacher berate all of us about how we were not good enough. About twenty of us were in the class and we bonded over his ridiculous teaching style. Behind his back, we were all rolling our eyes because he did not teach, just demeaned. But the thing is, his message seeped in. I started believing I could not make art. I started doubting my creativity. He was the expert. What did I know?

Up until that year, I had taken an art or music class nearly every year of my life. After that, I did not do a single artistic thing for five years. He almost ended my artistic and creative pursuits. Almost.

Ten years after that experience, I found myself lecturing to art and quilt guilds about creativity. During my lectures, I often shared the story about the art class. After every talk, at least one person, and usually several, would come up to me and say, "I have the same story. My experience was in fifth grade." Or seventh grade or tenth grade. Nearly everyone I know has had someone at some point in their life tell them they are not creative. It may have been a teacher, a parent, a boss, but always someone they believed had more wisdom than they did. The message gets buried deep in our psyches and we believe it, especially if it happens at a young, impressionable age.

Then all those people who were told they were not creative grew up and entered the workforce. Nearly every job needs some creativity. Yet those employees have no idea how to be creative. Not only do they not have the skills for it, but they also deeply believe they cannot be creative. This is a big problem and hinders innovation around the world.

This book is not about making art. It is about creativity. While creativity and artistic skills can be related, they are also two separate things. Whether or not you had negative experiences with art or creativity as a kid, certainly some of your employees have. You will learn ways you and your team can move past those old beliefs and develop your present-day creativity.

This book is also about teams, because they are critical for innovation. You will learn how to guide your team to be more creative and develop innovative solutions to real challenges. We need your creativity and your team's creativity because you have so much to offer.

The Global Need for Team Creativity

In 2010, IBM did a study on complexity in the workplace and interviewed more than 1,500 CEOs and other business leaders from sixty countries.[1] The CEOs cited creativity as the most important leadership quality for navigating the upcoming complexities facing the world. They also consistently said that one feature defines organizations that maneuver change well—creativity.

The World Economic Forum published the *Future of Jobs Report* in 2020 and listed the top ten skills needed for 2025.[2] Innovation was number one, creativity was number five, and ideation was number ten. The report also indicated that half of employees would need reskilling and upskilling to gain new skills needed for their jobs. This could include training on how to be more creative. Fortunately, reskilling and upskilling are great investments, and most employers expect to see a return in one year or less. *Forbes* simply says, "Creativity Is the New Black."[3]

Creativity needs to come from all levels of the organization, not just the top leadership. In fact, ideas from the bottom up are sometimes the most valuable.[4] Sometimes individuals come up with an idea, but they can rarely implement it on their own. More often, creative solutions are developed through collaborative conversations, interactive dialogue, and the deep teamwork needed for creativity. Given the complexities in organizations, teams are critical for innovation to take hold.

Creativity Is Innate

A year after college I was leading wilderness trips for teenagers in Colorado. During a rare day off, I wandered into a bookstore in Steamboat Springs. I bought two books about the creative process: *The Artist's Way* by Julia Cameron and *Life, Paint, and Passion* by Michele Cassou and Stewart Cubley. When I look back on that day I have no idea why I found those books, but something drew me to them. They shifted my thinking. I started seeing that creativity is about the process as much as or even more than the product. I learned that creativity emerges from doing the work. It is not spontaneous or magical. It is not that some of us are born with it and others are not. Creativity is innate to humans. We all have it. It is like a well. It is just a matter of tapping into it and letting it seep out.

After reading those books I started digging deep into understanding creativity. Two years later, I was a graduate student at the University of New Hampshire and taught my first workshop on creativity. It was a small group that met weekly for five weeks. I facilitated exercises and assigned them homework to bring out their creativity. I was not sure it would work. In some ways, I was making it up as I went. But the conversations were rich and the results were energizing. Students said they felt more creative. I was hooked.

For years, I kept experimenting with the best ways to teach creativity. At first, I only focused on individual creativity, but then I started combining my background in experiential education and team development with teaching creativity to teams. I learned about a process called creative problem solving (which I will expand on later). I studied design thinking and human-centered design. In 2011, I started my PhD at Antioch University with the intent to research creativity in teams. By then, I had already led creativity workshops with many teams, and I was giddy with possibility.

Be deliberate to be creative.

I saw that teams could indeed become more creative with training. Developing creativity in teams could reverse the mangled messages so many of us received about creativity. If we reversed those messages and developed team skills around creativity, teams could effectively navigate the complexities the organizations were facing and bring positive change to their customers, clients, communities, and even the world.

Deliberate Creativity Together

As an innovation consultant, I have taught creativity skills to thousands of leaders in organizations big and small over the last twenty-five years. Sometimes when I am planning a workshop I get a bit nervous because I think, "These are top executives for a billion-dollar company. They are going to know this stuff already." Or "These are accomplished engineers with patents to their name. What could I possibly teach them?" I would develop the workshop with lots of contingency plans for additional content or pivoting if needed. But every time, the groups embrace the content and experience. They do not already know the material. They are intrigued and energized to learn new perspectives on creativity. They generate loads of new ideas and later implement the best ones. It is fun to watch.

I am going to teach you the same process I teach in those workshops. It is based on my research, which was built on the research of hundreds of others. Through my dissertation, I identified three elements that teams need if they want to be creative together and if they want to innovate on demand (team purpose, team dynamics, and team creative process). I will share with you the process for how to lead your team to build their skills to be more creative together. I will also share a few of the activities I teach my clients so that you can apply the principles of deliberate creativity with your teams.

Through my research and consulting work, I have learned so much about creativity and innovation. The underlying premise is that creativity will not happen by accident. You are not going to just wake up one day with a brilliant solution for an unknown problem. It is only through deliberate work that you will be more creative. A process and a system for being creative have emerged from how we as humans naturally solve problems. I call it the Deliberate Creative Team system. The good news is that you can learn this system and use it in your work. If you apply that system with your team, the results can be mind-blowing!

If you are a leader who wants your team to be more creative, you are in the right place. We have the same goal. I want your team to be more creative because I know that creative teams produce innovative results that positively change the world.

Maybe you see the potential in your team. Maybe you know that by collectively solving your problems you can change people's lives. Maybe you have felt stuck and have wondered if there is a better way to innovate. There is and I will show you.

I invite you to join me and embrace my mantra—be deliberate to be creative.

If you put in the work, the possibilities are endless. As you will see in the book, creative teams solve problems that do not have a known solution. They design, invent, develop, and create solutions that change lives, even save lives.

1

Why You Need to Innovate Now

MARCH 10, 1973, was a good day for Frances for two reasons. She was getting married to Ron, and she did not have a headache. For the previous fifteen years, Frances had suffered headaches that continued to grow in severity. Some days there was no pain. Other days were so bad she could only sit in a dark, quiet room for hours and stay very still.

Back in high school, she had started seeing doctors to figure out what was causing the problem. Every single doctor dismissed her. They told her to just take it easy and decrease stress in her life. In 1961, during her freshman year of college, one doctor at a well-respected university hospital looked at her and said, "If you are worried you have a brain tumor, you don't."

Frances's frustration and pain grew to the point that she could barely cope. Finally, a few months after her and Ron's wedding, in a state of desperation, Frances and her parents drove a motor home from Orlando, Florida, to Rochester, Minnesota, to visit Mayo Clinic, which had a worldwide reputation as one of the best hospitals. Filled with hope and trepidation, they traveled over 1,400 miles seeking answers.

Mayo Clinic was opened in 1889 by the Sisters of Saint Francis and Drs. William and Charles Mayo.[1] From the beginning their approach to medicine was different. They designed an environment that was open, collaborative, and deeply dedicated to learning. Their drive to provide the best care led to continual innovation that influenced health care around the world. The focus was always on the patient, not about being right or about egos. Doctors with various specialties were assigned to a patient, and they consulted together to determine the diagnosis and treatment. Patients did not travel around the campus to the doctors; they stayed in one location and doctors came to them. When Mayo Clinic doctors consulted on Frances's symptoms, they suspected she had a brain tumor.[2]

In 1973 testing for a brain tumor involved a myelogram. The patient is strapped onto a special table that rotates. Fluid is injected into their spine. As the table rotates, the fluid moves to different parts of the body. If the fluid hits a tumor, the patient experiences pain. When the fluid hit the back of Frances's skull, the pain was so intense that she vomited.

The MRI machine had not yet been invented, but the EMI scanner had. It was the first machine to allow 3D views of the brain, and it would soon revolutionize medicine. In 1973 there were only two EMI scanners in the world. One was in the United Kingdom, where it had been invented, and the other was at Mayo Clinic.[3]

The EMI scanner had only been at Mayo for a few weeks, and they wanted to test it on Frances. Later when Frances was asked what it was like to be in the EMI scanner, she said, "There was nothing to it. I just lay on a table in the dark. It wasn't painful at all." The results showed the same thing as the myelogram. There was a brain tumor.

On July 19, 1973, Dr. Richard H. Miller, assisted by Dr. David Piepgras, removed Frances's tumor. In the middle of the surgery, they tested the tumor for cancer.

By 1906, 4,770 operations had already been performed at Mayo Clinic, more than at any hospital in the United States.[4] As early as 1893, it had an impressive surgery success rate of 98 percent,[5] and soon doctors around the world traveled to the little town in Minnesota to learn from the Mayo brothers, who were continually looking at problems and devising new solutions.

For instance, an early medical challenge the Mayo brothers struggled with was that when surgically removing a tumor, they would have to sew the patient back up without knowing if the tumor was cancerous.[6] It might take weeks for the tests to determine if cancer was present, and this could lead to a second or even third surgery, putting the patient at greater risk. To address this, in 1905 the Mayo brothers hired pathologist Louis Wilson. His job was to figure out a new way to quickly test cells for cancer. Months later, after countless attempts, he had a solution. With his new technique, it took only two minutes to determine if cells were cancerous. That meant surgeons could remove a tumor and test it for cancer while a patient was still in surgery. The results would give them valuable information about their next steps while the patient was still under anesthesia.

Seven decades later, Drs. Miller and Piepgras removed Frances's tumor and it was taken next door to the lab to test for cancer. The tumor was benign.

But the tumor was about the size of a lemon. Taking it easy and decreasing stress would not have resolved Frances's massive headaches!

Two days after the surgery Frances asked Dr. Miller if the surgery had been necessary. He said, "Yes. Pretty soon you were going to go to sleep and not wake up." The surgery saved her life.

Two weeks later Frances and her parents were back home in Orlando, and Frances was feeling well enough that she helped Ron pressure-wash the roof of their house. Post-op recovery was going well.

I am forever grateful to Mayo Clinic because Frances and Ron later went on to have three kids. I was their first. As I write this book, my mom is still alive and well and had no long-term effects from the tumor.

Without the removal of the tumor, my mom would have died long before I was born. It is because of Mayo's innovative approach to medicine that I exist. For me, innovation is personal.

For Mayo Clinic, innovation has always been at the core of their identity. Today, it is listed as one of their top eight values and they practice it every day. Because of their innovative approach to medicine and their drive for improvement, they have saved millions of lives and their inventions and discoveries have affected nearly every human on Earth.

Today, Mayo employs seven thousand active inventors, and they just broke $1 billion in revenue from their inventions.[7] Mayo Clinic is a great example of an organization that focuses on identifying problems and finding creative solutions.

How can an organization like Mayo Clinic continue to innovate for over a century? How do they produce groundbreaking results and become the sought-after resource when no one else can help? How have they been able to save millions of lives through their innovations?

Mayo Clinic understands that innovation is a system.

Specific strategies, techniques, and tools make up the system for creativity. Creativity and innovation emerge by following a deliberate process, a system that allows individuals and teams to identify challenges, generate new ideas, develop those ideas, and then test and implement them.

You might not be working in a field that focuses on life-saving work. Whether you are in accounting, engineering, education, or zoology, innovation can lead to positive change. Innovation is about solving real problems and leads to real solutions for real people. You might not be trying to invent a new way to test for cancer cells or invent a product that changes the world, but even small changes make a big difference. Maybe you want to change the communication practices in your restaurant to create a smoother, more efficient experience for staff and customers; lead your office to be more inclusive and open so staff can collaborate at a deeper level; design a system to keep students safe from gun violence at school; create a company that produces locally made, sustainable clothing at scale while still earning a profit; decrease waste within your company to save money and the environment; or eradicate biased hiring practices and pay inequities at your organization.

In all of these examples, and a myriad of others, there is no one right answer or one known solution. Solving problems without a known solution requires creativity. If you want to be creative, you need to follow a deliberate system.

In the last few years, I have had the privilege to work with many clients, including Mayo Clinic, and teach them the Deliberate Creative Team system. The system is based on my original research on creativity in teams and builds on decades of research and practical experiences from other creativity experts. In this book, I will teach you the same system. You will learn how to guide your team to be innovative whenever you need.

If you want to be creative, **you need to follow a deliberate system.**

Why Bother with Creativity?

Creativity involves identifying challenges, generating ideas, developing those ideas into viable solutions, and implementing the new solutions. Yes, it is a lot of work. So why bother? Because the results can be remarkable. Does being remarkable matter? It matters because when things are changing around you if you are not able to adapt and innovate, you get left behind.

So many aspects of our world are experiencing rapid change, but isn't that always the case? I chuckle when I see an article from the 1940s, '60s, or '90s and it says, "We are in a time of unprecedented change." I think we will feel this way for the rest of our human existence.

You may have heard the phrase "innovate or die." (Its exact origins are unclear.) I think a more accurate phrase is "innovate or slowly wither away." If you become stagnant and choose not to innovate, most likely you will not go out of business overnight or become irrelevant tomorrow, but give it a few months or a few years. Or in the case of the department store Sears, you might struggle for two decades until you declare bankruptcy with an $11-billion debt!

A Lesson from Sears

The story of Sears fascinates me because it was a company built on innovation, and it continued to innovate for over one hundred years. Then it got complacent.

At the turn of the twentieth century, the United States was emerging from the industrial revolution and cities had become bustling hubs of commerce. However, millions of Americans still lived on rural land with little access to the cities. Before cars and roads were commonplace, a big problem for those in rural America was gaining access to goods that were sold in stores in the cities. Without cars or even roads, getting to a store to buy items such as clothes, household goods, tools, sewing machines, and linens was a significant journey. What might be a one-hour drive today would have been a two- to three-day trek on a horse.

The US Postal Service played a critical role in solving this problem. As the United States grew, so did the Postal Service. By the early 1900s the Postal Service would deliver letters and packages to anywhere in the country. (This was before Alaska and Hawaii were states.)

Sears, Roebuck and Co., a department store in Chicago, Illinois, was keen to capitalize on this developing system of delivering goods. In 1897 Sears launched its first catalog. By taking advantage of the Postal Service it could get products to people anywhere in the country. By 1909 the catalog was over five hundred pages. You could buy anything from it—a house, a wedding dress, guns, kitchen implements, hairbrushes, shoes, watches, and much more. The first house I ever owned was a Sears home built in the 1940s. It is still standing strong.

Sears continued to be known for innovation well into the 1980s. Allstate Insurance, the Discover credit card, Coldwell Banker Real Estate, Kenmore appliances, and Diehard batteries were all spawned from Sears. If you were interested in innovation, Sears was a great place to work.

As consumer patterns in the United States shifted, shopping malls increased in popularity. Sears was often an anchor store and by the mid-1990s had over three thousand stores. Meanwhile, the catalog was decreasing in popularity, and by 1993 it closed its catalog division to respond to the shifting needs and trends of the country.[8] Unfortunately, the company needed to do more to stay relevant.

Sears stopped turning a profit in 2010.[9] Although at the turn of the twentieth century it had done a great job of capitalizing on the prevailing innovation of the Postal Service, a century later it failed to take advantage of the internet. The company could have easily become the Amazon of our day. Instead, it got complacent, ignored the trends, and focused on doing more of the same. By 2017, the chain had dwindled to 695 stores.[10] In October 2018, the company filed for bankruptcy. An American institution was lost. As of April 2024, there were eleven Sears stores left. Its inability or unwillingness to innovate meant it slowly withered away and became irrelevant.

Shifts in Higher Ed

Higher education is experiencing rapid change, and some colleges are already starting to see a fate similar to Sears's. Students are questioning if college is important and many are opting for another route. Even though many public and private schools are seeing a decline in enrollment, it is the small private colleges that are suffering the most. Their tuition is expensive and they rely on donors to provide scholarships and fund operations.

Dr. Jay Roberts, the provost of Warren Wilson College in Asheville, North Carolina, said that with their current business model, costs per student significantly exceed revenues each year.[11] That is not sustainable. Something has to change. If the college cannot get creative and design innovative solutions, it risks closing its doors, despite its long history that began in 1894. It is not the only school in this position; college closings are increasing as more and more institutions wrestle with a failing business model.

In March 2024, the president and board of Northland College in Ashland, Wisconsin, announced that it would be closing if it did not receive $12 million in funding in the next twenty-three days.[12] The faculty council elected an ad hoc response committee of five members. Their assignment was to respond to the threat of imminent closure. Recognizing this as an all-hands-on-deck situation, outdoor education professor Dr. Elizabeth Andre and the four other committee members decided this required more than drafting a communication response.[13] The team led a group of dedicated faculty, staff, students, and community members to develop a new path forward. They engaged hundreds of people to provide iterative input on the new plan. They soon noticed that the more people who added input to the plan, the better it got. They called it the True Northland vision.

Within days they had developed a new plan that included restructuring the entire campus, slimming down spending in some areas and beefing it up in others, and opening up the beautiful campus to the community. They proposed a balanced budget that would work even if they saw a 40 percent drop in enrollment!

The process that the large, inclusive group went through in such a short time is a stellar example of innovation. Andre said, "That team was the best performing group I have ever been a part of." My favorite part is that one day a group of students who believed deeply in the school and saw the long hours the faculty were putting into the plan made a delicious lunch for all the faculty and staff who were working through the budget details!

It remains to be seen if the college president and board will be interested in making these changes and adopting the new plan. As of this writing, Northland's fate is unclear.

Nimble Nonprofits

North Carolina Outward Bound School (NCOBS) needed to diversify its offerings. Its staple programs of nine- to twenty-eight-day wilderness courses were no longer fully serving the organization's populations. Leadership wanted to provide more options. Sarah Goldman, the program director for professional programs, had been in her job for ten days when the COVID-19 pandemic hit.[14] She barely had her feet under her when she needed to get creative and make drastic changes.

Goldman met with some other staff members and started mapping out ideas. They quickly recognized that the four pillars that framed all their programs—craftsmanship, self-reliance, physical fitness, and compassion—could be taught virtually. Sarah was also a private adventure-racing coach and was used to working with clients virtually. She was familiar with the possibilities of online platforms. She sent an email to her supervisor telling him about their ideas to launch a virtual program. He replied with enthusiastic support.

Soon they launched a couple of pilot offerings and before long they were up and running. Participants were thrilled! Clients ranging from big corporations to local middle schools to international nonprofits signed up for the virtual program offerings with NCOBS. Eventually, Sarah and another staff member enrolled in a course I offered called Leading Engaging Virtual Meetings and further elevated NCOBS's virtual facilitation. Their virtual programs brought in $107,000 in the first year and significantly boosted the nonprofit's budget.[15]

In contrast, similar schools had the same opportunities to pivot. Instead, they held tight to their identities and traditions. They did not change and now they are struggling financially.

AS A LEADER, if you can respond to change with a creative lens, you will thrive. However, if you are not able and willing to be creative and innovate when needed, you risk becoming irrelevant and losing customers, clients, or students. Your finances will suffer. Your mission will suffer. I promise you our world will continue to change. If you cannot respond to that change, your organization will slowly wither away.

I do not believe the adage that people do not like change. Sometimes leaders tell me they cannot make changes because their staff do not like change. There is more to it than that. We invite change into our lives all the time. We get married, have kids, go on vacation to new places, and change jobs and careers. The world is changing primarily because of humans. As a species, we are excellent at change. We cause it. Some of the changes we cause are harmful, such as environmental degradation and pollution. Many of the changes we create are positive, such as the invention of electricity, the global infra-structure we have built, the internet that enables us to connect with others around the world, and chocolate chip cookies.

When I ask my clients why they put off making changes and what gets in the way of them being creative, they say things like:

- There is not enough time.
- We have too many other priorities.
- There is not enough money.
- We do not have enough ideas.
- We have lots of ideas, but it is too hard to pick the best idea.
- It is overwhelming to attempt creativity.
- I do not know where to start.
- I overthink and get stuck.
- There is no support from leadership.
- I'm afraid of criticism, especially if the creative ideas do not work.
- My own mindset. I do not think I am creative.
- It is hard to see the impact, so it feels pointless.
- It is scary.

Creativity
is novelty
that is
valuable.

When situations get dire, we start to see how useless our excuses are. What if we started making changes now instead of waiting until a crisis happens?

Creativity versus Innovation

We use the words "creativity" and "innovation" a lot, so let's clarify what these words mean.

For decades, in the field of creativity research, there was a debate about the definition of "creativity." Researchers finally came to a consensus with a robust and meaningful definition that works: "Creativity is the interaction among aptitude, process, and environment by which an individual or group produces a perceptible product that is both novel and useful as defined within a social context."[16]

Simply put, creativity is novelty that is useful or valuable. It is solving problems in a new way. That's it.

It is not about art or your ability to draw. Being creative just means you generate new ideas and turn them into a useful product. Think of "product" in a broad sense. It could refer to software, a process, system, theory, or physical product. Same with "useful." "Useful" is in the eye of the beholder and could include something classically practical, like a stapler, or a piece of art that evokes emotions. I like using the word "valuable" instead of "useful." It has a slightly broader interpretation. I have found that "useful" tends to trip up my clients as well, so my working definition of creativity is as follows: Creativity is novelty that is valuable.

To talk about creativity in teams, we also need to discuss innovation. Again, after years of debate and numerous attempts to define the word "innovation," Anahita Baregheh and her team of researchers offered a clear definition: "The multi-stage process whereby organizations transform ideas into new/improved products, services or processes, to advance, compete and differentiate themselves successfully in their marketplace."[17] This is similar to creativity but with a focus on organizations and the added element of financial impact. The term "innovation" is used more often in business, technology, and engineering fields, whereas "creativity" is used more in the humanities, arts, and education.

For instance, we often say that artist Georgia O'Keeffe was creative, whereas former Apple CEO Steve Jobs was innovative. They both followed a creative process, and they both produced results that were novel and valuable. They also had a profound impact on the world, which is not critical to creativity but is a nice bonus in this case. While it is technically correct to say Georgia O'Keeffe was innovative and Steve Jobs was creative, because of the fields they worked in, we tend to express it differently.

The bottom line: Both creativity and innovation are the result of a process that leads to a product that is novel and valuable.

There are so many misconceptions about creativity and innovation, and I will address several of them in this book. Getting clear on the definitions debunks a couple of myths.

"I'm Not Creative Because I Can't Draw"

For nearly twenty years when leading a workshop or delivering a keynote, I have asked participants if they think they are creative. The moment that surprised me most was when I asked a room full of artists if they thought they were creative. Only half of them raised their hand! Many people do not see themselves as creative (although I have noticed that this has improved over the last decade, perhaps because, as a society, our understanding of creativity is improving).

Our perception of our own creativity matters. Psychologists call this "creative self-efficacy." Those with a higher level of creative self-efficacy, those who believe they can be creative, tend to produce more creative results.[18] If you do not believe you are creative, you probably will not be. If your team members do not believe they are creative, they will not be and your team's results will suffer.

I rarely work with companies where the staff needs drawing skills. Yet so many adults think they are not creative because they cannot draw. I know I just gave you the definition of creativity, but I want to be crystal clear here: Creativity is not about your ability to draw. If you struggle with sketching stick figures or think of "draw" as a bad four-letter word, do not worry. If you grew up attending a mainstream school in the United States, you probably had little to no instruction in how to draw. Most likely you had an occasional art class and even more rarely did the class focus specifically on drawing. At its most basic level, drawing is a combination of curved and straight lines put together in a certain way. Imagine if we taught kindergarteners the alphabet in the same way we teach drawing. We would expect them to recognize and recreate letters on the first or second attempt. If they did not get it right away, we would tell them to pursue something else in life. We would live in a nation of illiterate people! It would be a huge mess. Drawing is a skill that you can develop if you want, but it is not related to your ability to be creative.

We teach kids to read and write letters (in other words, draw the alphabet) through practice, repetition, and feedback over a several-year span. This is essentially how we learn most skills. The same is required for the two skills of learning to draw and learning to be creative. If you want to learn to draw, excellent books and courses can teach you how. If you are not interested, let it go and move on. But let's distinguish drawing skills from the act of creativity and focus on developing your ability to solve problems creatively.

"Creativity Is Only about Generating Ideas"

Another common misconception is that creativity is just about generating ideas. Sometimes leaders dismiss generating lots of ideas because they see ideas as fluffy, irrelevant, outrageous, and pointless, essentially a waste of time. Ideas alone are relatively worthless. It is what you do with those ideas that matters. Creativity is about solving problems. To solve a problem, you must implement a solution. Creativity and innovation both involve implementation.

Creativity is not a magical, mystical, mysterious muse that visits the chosen few in their dreams. No. It is not fluffy and cute. It is not a nice-to-have. It is a critical part of business success. If you want to thrive, learn to apply deliberate creativity.

Innovate on Demand

As a leader, your job is to guide your team to identify problems, find new ideas, develop solutions, and implement those solutions that lead to positive change. It is a big challenge, but quite doable—because if you understand how team creativity works and you know how to bring out the best in your team members, then you can lead them to collaborate toward true innovation. In this book, I will show you how to do all of that. Soon, you and your team will be able to innovate on demand and know how to tackle any new problem.

If you understand that creativity is a system and you know and follow that system, you will be more innovative. There are many barriers to the process and a lot to learn, but I am here to guide you. I am going to teach you how to lead your team to be more creative so that you can solve real problems, serve others, and make the world a better place. By the end of this book, you will know how to lead your team to innovate whenever they want.

2

Not by Magic
or Chance

E ARLY IN MY CAREER I worked in student affairs at the
University of Wisconsin. My office was part of a bigger
programming unit, and twelve of us met every two weeks
to discuss our work. One day, while we sat around a big
wooden conference table, a teammate, Maria, said she was
feeling stuck on a problem and asked if we could brainstorm
some new ideas with her.

I heard the word "brainstorm," stopped my doodling, sat
up a bit taller, and grinned. I loved brainstorming. This was
my jam! I was all in.

Maria explained her problem, and we started spitballing
ideas. Maria listened as teammates shared the first three ideas.
She nodded and added a comment or two after each one. It
seemed to be going well until a teammate threw out idea
number four, and Phil, a veteran of the team, shouted, "No!
We cannot do that. We did that in 1985 and it was a complete
disaster."

I burst out laughing. It was such a great joke!

Phil glared at me.

Oh. He was not joking.

I shrank back a little. My mind was whizzing. My internal dialogue was rapid-firing questions. "What is going on? Is he serious? I was a child in 1985. He cannot possibly think that just because something was tried nearly two decades ago that we would have the same result today. Maybe we could learn from that experience and try again. Why is he even saying anything? We are just brainstorming."

Everyone fell silent. Tension rose.

Maria finally said, "Okay. I will not try that idea. Any others?"

No one said anything. Maria was on her own to solve this one.

I left that meeting livid. Back in our office, my boss and I vented about Phil. Our team should have been able to provide a lot of worthwhile ideas for Maria to solve her problem. We had more ideas in us, and Phil went and ruined it. Our team was a mess. We maintained the status quo well, but new ideas were often met with resistance.

If you observed our meetings, you would see that we got along fairly well. Meetings were calm and organized, but there was no energy or drive for innovation. When I talked with other team members individually, they had lots of ideas and passion, but they felt stymied because of the culture within the team. I was so frustrated because I could see the potential. We needed to develop a stronger culture within our team so we could be more creative and produce innovative results for the university and, most importantly, for the students we worked with. Thirty years earlier, back in the 1970s, our unit had a national reputation for innovation and cutting-edge programs. Now, in the new century, we were riding on that thirty-year-old reputation and growing stale. As a staff, many of us had great ideas that could have pushed us to be more innovative and provide better experiences for students, but instead we were stagnant.

That meeting was just one example of many meetings I have been in with nearly identical results. Have you had this experience? Have you been in a brainstorming session that failed miserably? If so, you may have felt the same tension I did, followed by the same disappointment.

Maybe you were the one to shoot down the idea. I sheepishly raise my hand and admit I have made that mistake too. Despite my drive to be creative, I have inadvertently knocked down ideas. I have jumped in too soon or made assumptions about an idea without asking questions.

Fortunately, that day in our staff meeting was not all bad. That meeting, and many others like it, sparked a passion in me to figure out why some teams are highly creative and others are not.

What type of potential do you see in your team? Is your organization facing significant problems that your team can address? Perhaps you can imagine the new products or services your team could design for clients. Maybe your team will develop new efficiencies to do their work better. If your team can be more creative, what would this mean for you, for them, for the organization, and for those you serve?

At the time of this incident with Phil, I had been studying personal creativity for a few years. I had read lots of books and even taught a few classes. I dabbled in making art in a variety of mediums. I wondered if I could figure out how our team could be more creative together. I was excited to blend my curiosity about teams and creativity.

And then, about eight months later, the real aha moment happened.

At the end of the school year, Phil hosted our team at his house for a little celebration. As we casually relaxed in his backyard and ate pizza, I met his wife and ten-year-old son. I learned that Phil played the guitar and had been in local theater productions. As I listened to his son talk about some of the things they did together, I saw a completely different side of Phil. I saw his creativity. I was surprised. I had no idea Phil enjoyed being creative.

He had been working at the university for twenty years. When he walked through the doors of our building each day, something was stripping away his creativity. This was a big problem because Phil was not the only one leaving his creativity at the door. We all were. My sense of urgency increased. How many other teams were having this same problem? As I started learning more and paying attention to teams, I realized the problem was huge. Monumental. Worldwide.

I stayed in that job for less than three years, but I often wonder what positive impact our team might have had on the students we worked with had we been able to produce more innovative results. What if we had deliberately worked to be more creative together? What if every team could be highly creative? What impact would that have on our communities and the world?

That experience with Phil was more than two decades ago. I have spent twenty-five years researching creativity in teams. I have taught hundreds of teams and thousands of people to be more creative and effective. I have learned two important things that are the foundation of all my work:

- Creativity is a teachable, learnable skill that is available to nearly everyone.

- When we follow a system for creativity, we produce more creative and innovative results.

There was another layer to Phil's story that I did not see then. I will share more on that later.

Creativity Is about Solving Problems

Now you know that creativity is not about drawing; it is a skill, a process, and a system. It is also less about innate ability; rather it is about working intentionally to solve problems and create new solutions to meaningful questions. It is about thinking in a new way and accepting that there is no one right answer. To develop these skills, you and your team members must learn how creativity works. Unfortunately, you may be starting at a disadvantage.

In 2012, Dr. Diane Baker and Dr. Susan Baker wrote an article comparing MFA programs to MBA programs and argued that teaching creativity to business students is critical.[1] I agree. Creativity is an essential skill for business students because it is an essential skill for businesses.

A master in fine arts (MFA) degree is a terminal degree for artists, writers, and actors who want to dive deep into their artistic pursuits and push the boundaries of their creative potential. Students are encouraged to explore different techniques, mediums, and perspectives, and the curriculum is centered on the creative process. Built on decades of research that has shown creativity is a learnable skill,[2] MFA programs are designed around the premise that creativity can be taught.

Most master in business administration (MBA) programs are focused on analytical and decision-making skills. Their marketing material claims that they will foster innovation in their students, but there is often little focus on developing creativity. In his 2010 TED Talk, Tom Wujec explained a classic team development activity called the Marshmallow Challenge.[3] Teams have eighteen minutes to build a free-standing tower using only dry sticks of spaghetti, masking tape, and a string. The tower must support a marshmallow at the top. He has facilitated this activity with thousands of teams and found that among the groups that perform the best are recent

Creativity is a teachable, learnable skill that is available to everyone.

graduates of kindergarten. Among the groups that perform the worst are recent graduates of business school.

I often use the marshmallow activity or similar activities with teams and have found the same results. In one situation, I was leading a team-building activity that involved hula hoops and lots of tennis balls. The solution required groups to look at the problem in a slightly new way and challenge their assumptions. Most groups figure it out in about three rounds. Fifth graders often solve it in minutes. I worked with one group of MBA students a few years ago, and after forty-five minutes they still had not figured it out! They were so frustrated that we had to stop the exercise. They did not have the skills to work together and look at the problem from a new angle.

A typical process for MFA students is to pose a problem they want to address through their art. It could be a societal issue such as racism or gun violence, a more personal matter like the relationships between mothers and daughters, or an artistic dilemma such as the interplay between shape and line. Then they explore how to best represent that in their art. They may research the issue and grapple with what exactly they are trying to say, then generate lots of ideas in the form of sketches or notes. From there they develop some of the best ideas further, either through mock-ups, prototypes, or smaller pieces. Eventually, they bring it together in a final piece of art or writing. With these steps, they are essentially moving through a process of solving problems creatively. There is a focus on experimenting and seeing what works, scrapping ideas that fail, and keeping those that are a good fit.

I have a few friends who have recently gone back to school to get an MBA. When I ask them how their classes are going, they shrug and make a few comments about how irrelevant it is to their work. They laugh about how pointless it seems, but now they are committed and will go through the motions to get the three letters after their name.

This is not a slam on MBA programs, as I am sure some of them are excellent. The point here is that we are not great at teaching how to solve problems creatively, even though it is critical. Solving problems creatively is the hallmark of good business. If you want your business to succeed, you need to do this well.

Creativity Must Be Taught

Back in the 1950s a prevalent belief was that leaders were born, not made. I am grateful that as a society we now believe the evidence that leadership skills are built over time through training, experience, feedback, and reflection. This has led to better leaders and improved leadership practices. Likewise, our beliefs about creativity need to catch up with the research, which is crystal clear: Creativity training works.

In 1972, creativity researcher and educational psychologist E. Paul Torrance from the University of Georgia compiled the research on creativity training in children. He conducted the first meta-analysis on the topic and compared the results of 142 studies. A meta-analysis is a research process where the data from numerous independent studies are analyzed to determine trends and themes across the research. It is a powerful research tool.

That in 1972 there were already 142 studies testing creativity training on children is shocking to me. Over fifty years ago, we had already compiled that much research, yet we still do not teach creativity in schools and most people believe that your creative ability is genetic and cannot be learned. Sigh.

Torrance found that creativity training does indeed increase creativity. In that first meta-analysis, creative problem solving (which you will learn about in chapter 6) was the most common method and had a 91 percent success rate. Fast-forward to this century and other meta-analyses found creative problem solving training to be effective with children and adults, including in business contexts.[4]

Not only can creativity be taught, but it must be taught. Although we are all hard-wired to be creative, saying that is like saying we are hard-wired for language. Nearly everyone can learn to speak, write, and read, but language still requires learning. This is why English is a required class every year from kindergarten until high school graduation. If only creativity were also required learning.

Creativity training positively impacts communication, the fluency and originality of ideas, the ability to evaluate and implement ideas, attitudes toward divergent thinking, as well as the financial bottom line.[5] For instance, one study reported that a manufacturing plant saw a decrease in expenditures of $40,000 per week based on one change that came about from creativity training.[6] By any measure, that is an impressive savings.

Another study delivered creativity training to half of the 346 city employees in Orange County, California. In only eight months, city officials reported nearly $600,000 in new revenues and $3.5 million in innovative expenditure reductions. They attributed this financial gain to the new ideas developed by employees after their creativity training. Part of this was attributed to a change in culture that was brought about by the training. Specifically, "employees seemed more willing to share new ideas, and managers seemed more willing to hear them."[7]

I interviewed Tom Heck, a consultant to start-ups that specialize in K-12 STEM education. He has trained thousands of K-12 educators around the world on how to use an innovative teaching tool called Makey Makey in their classrooms.

Tom said that nearly every teacher he has worked with under-stands the importance of innovation but also recognizes how bad we are at teaching it. He said, "The system is designed to not promote the teaching of innovation and creativity."[8]

As a society, we have gotten ourselves into a real pickle. We all know that creativity matters, yet we do very little to promote it or teach it to kids. Now those kids are adults who are working in your company. As a leader, you have a particu-lar conundrum. You want your team to be creative, but few of your people have been taught this skill. Therefore, they need training and development of their creativity skills.

In later chapters, we will explore how your team might develop skills for creativity and innovation. Getting inten-tional about creativity starts with learning the system and then teaching your team how to be deliberate creatives so they can innovate anytime.

The Deliberate Creative Spectrum

A team's ability to innovate falls along a spectrum. Before looking at the system of deliberate creativity, let's consider where you and your team are right now so that you know what you need to do to get to where you want to go.

The Deliberate Creative Spectrum describes five levels that teams fall along. As teams move up the ladder, their creativ-ity grows, and their impact increases. While most businesses think about impact as financial, the impact also might include cultural, social, environmental, or academic influence. Below is an explanation of each of the levels and how a team at that level might affect an organization. As you are learning about these five levels, think about where your team might be.

THE DELIBERATE CREATIVE SPECTRUM

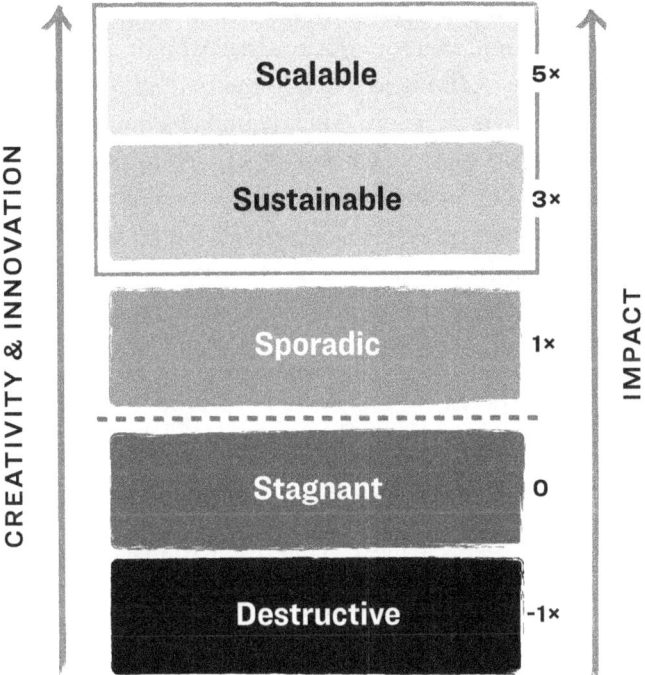

The Destructive Creative Team

Starting at the bottom level, destructive creative teams are destroying creative efforts. Team members quickly shoot down ideas in meetings, talk about the way things have always been done, and work to maintain the status quo. They may not intentionally be demolishing creativity. They might mean well, but fear of change drives their response. Whatever their intentions, the effect of their behavior is that new ideas are not pursued and therefore revenue is lost. For this example, let's say they nix an idea that had the potential to generate $500,000 in new income. Their team behavior has cost the company $500,000, which will be referred to as -1x. (Please insert a number for $500,000 that makes sense in your context.) How much revenue would a good idea generate for your organization? How much are lost ideas costing you?

You might be on a destructive creative team if:

- Team members regularly shoot down one another's ideas. Or ideas are not even requested or shared.

- Some team members may feel nervous or uncomfortable sharing ideas or commenting on ideas shared.

- The team seems to have no interest in trying to be creative.

- There seems to be resistance to all types of change.

- You feel less creative when you are with the team than in other situations.

- Your team has not implemented a new, positive change in a long time, or ever.

- Meetings do not feel open and collaborative, and they may be dominated by two or three people.

An important note here as you are evaluating your team: Not all teams need to be creative. While creativity is important, it is not needed in every context. However, the destructive team sabotages innovative progress. As you will learn next, stagnant teams are in a more neutral mode.

The Stagnant Creative Team

Up one level are teams that are stagnant in their creativity. They may be thriving in other aspects of their work. Perhaps they are highly productive or successful at sales, but they do not strive to be creative. They do not necessarily destroy creativity, but they are not contributing to it either. They are having neither a positive nor negative impact on innovative changes in the company. However, their lost potential can be quite expensive to a company. Their revenue from new ideas is zero. Many teams start at this level. In some cases, this is fine. If the team is designed to maintain the status quo, then being creative may not be important. However, be careful because new ideas and improvements can come from anywhere in an organization. Often frontline employees see things that managers do not see. You want to make sure they have a voice to share perspectives and new ideas that might increase efficiencies, bring in new revenue, and improve the organization.

You might be on a stagnant creative team if:

- Team members sometimes dismiss ideas too quickly.

- Ideas are asked for but then not truly considered. The act of trying to generate new ideas seems to be more of a formality than a true interest.

- Some team members may feel nervous or unmotivated to share ideas.

- Team members seem content with how things are and uninterested in changes.

Solving problems creatively is **the hallmark of good business.**

- Your team has not implemented a new, positive change in a long time.

- Meetings are primarily a report from each person. Team members may discuss small issues, but there is rarely true collaboration around a problem.

The Sporadic Creative Team

Above the dashed line in the graphic is where we start seeing positive results. The sporadic creative team strives to be creative, yet they do not always know what to do. They value creativity so they try various approaches, use their intuition, and sometimes have success that leads to positive changes. But they do not know why they were creative or how to do the same things again. They do not know and use a repeatable process, and their success in innovation is somewhat accidental. Innovation happens sometimes but not consistently. It is sporadic. Their successes are 1x, so in this example their new ideas may periodically bring in $500,000 of new revenue or saved expenses.

You might be on a sporadic creative team if:

- Team members seem to want to be creative, even if they do not quite know how.

- There are attempts to generate new ideas.

- You only use one method for generating new ideas, typically the classic brainstorming approach.

- Sometimes your team has new ideas that are implemented; other times the new ideas are ignored.

- There is a collective energy swell you feel when creative collaboration happens together.

The Sustainable Creative Team

The sustainable creative team uses a clear process to harness creativity. The process is reliable and repeatable, and team members understand how to apply it in a variety of contexts. Therefore, they can be creative and produce innovative results with consistency. They have the skills, the knowledge, and the process to innovate on demand. The impact on the organization is at least three times as much as that of the sporadic creative team. In our example, they are bringing in $1,500,000 in revenue or saved expenses.

You might be on a sustainable creative team if:

- Each team member knows how the creative process works.

- Because of previous successes, there is a collective motivation and drive to innovate.

- There is a collective energy and focus on being creative.

- The team is positioned to apply the creative process whenever it is needed. For instance, you have the space, time, and supplies available in advance.

- Team members understand their own strengths and preferences within the creative process and collaborate in a way that maximizes the results.

- You regularly produce innovative results that have a positive impact on the organization and beyond.

The Scalable Creative Team

The scalable creative team knows the creative process so well that its members can impact not only the colleagues and clients they directly work with, but also those in other parts of an organization. They become creative evangelists and a model team to follow. They teach others throughout the organization how creativity works. Their impact is at least five times that of the sporadic creative team. In this example, their impact is $2,500,000 or more. Very few teams reach this high level of performance.

You might be on a scalable creative team if:

- Your team's consistent innovative results have been recognized by others.

- You mentor, advise, or teach other teams how to be more creative.

- The innovative results have had a positive impact on the organization and beyond.

A Deliberate Creative Team has reached one of the top two levels in the diagram. They know and use a creative process that produces valuable results, and they have a clear purpose and strong team dynamics that lead to innovation.

In my experience with my clients, most teams are either stagnant or sporadic, especially without training in deliberate creativity. To move up the ladder to a higher level, your team needs to know and use a system for deliberate creativity. Your team needs a system so they can innovate more frequently, more consistently, and with more impact. Through my research I have developed the Deliberate Creative Team system so that you can innovate whenever you want.

The Deliberate Creative Team System

I was recently facilitating an ideation session for the advancement team of the North Carolina Outward Bound School. The seven staff members were focusing on how they might be more innovative in their development and marketing in the coming year. I taught them the concept that creativity is a skill that can and must be nurtured just like any other skill. As we talked about this, Walker, associate director of advancement operations, had a confused, pensive look on his face. I asked, "Walker, what are you thinking about?"

He said, "I'm just trying to wrap my head around this."

"Around what?" I asked.

"That creativity is a skill!"

I chuckled. The concept can be a bit mind-boggling at first, especially if you have always looked at other people as creative and not considered yourself as such. I find it freeing and exciting to know that if I want to be more creative, I just need to work at it. If I want my team to be more creative, then we need to work at it together.

Later, Walker and I talked further, and he said that beyond understanding that creativity is a skill, the idea of practicing creativity was new to him. Skills are something we can practice to improve.

In 2009 a group of researchers conducted a meta-analysis of 104 studies to determine what factors impact team creativity.[9] They reported in the *Journal of Applied Psychology* that the process in which teams engage and their relationships with each other are more important to their creative output than specific traits or backgrounds they bring to the group.[10] This is good news! This means that teams can influence their creativity. A team's ability to innovate is not based on team members' level of education or their personalities. Instead, it is based on how the team members work together, on the interactions and behaviors within the group, and on the process they use to innovate.

Knowing that the input from team members and their interactions with each other were the most important aspects of team creativity, I wanted to dig deeper. What, more specifically, leads to team innovation? Building on the previous seventy years of research, I conducted a study to look at what teams need to be creative together. After scouring the research, I identified the most likely elements of team creativity. I then crafted a survey, and over 830 people shared information about their teams. I worked in-depth with three teams to further test the results. The outcome was an assessment tool called the Deliberate Creative Team Scale,[11] which was tested for validity and reliability. The assessment turned out to be quite robust and will measure your team's behaviors related to creativity. I have since used the scale with many teams.

The results of the research show that teams need three factors to be creative:

- Team purpose
- Team dynamics
- Team creative process

DELIBERATE CREATIVE TEAMS

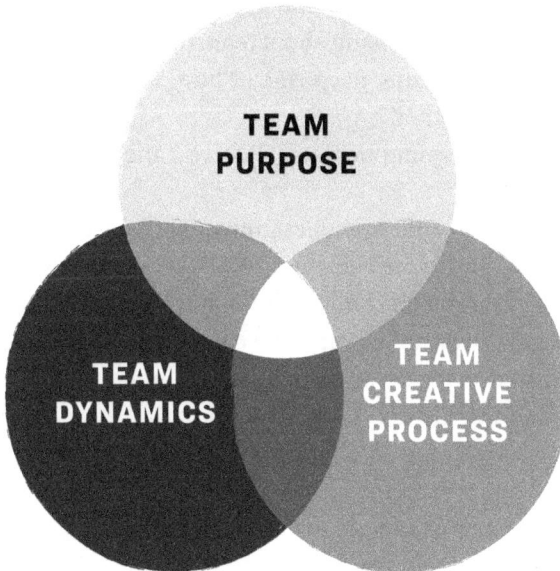

TEAM PURPOSE

TEAM DYNAMICS

TEAM CREATIVE PROCESS

These factors are team competencies that form the Deliberate Creative Team system. If your team can build their skills and strengths in these three areas, the results will be astounding. They will become a Deliberate Creative Team at the sustainable or scalable level. Your team will be able to innovate on demand.

Team Purpose

Team purpose is defined as a team's collective focus, shared goals, and commitment to reaching those goals. A clear sense of purpose is critical to the success of any team, whether striving to be creative or not.[12]

If a team is not clear about its purpose, how will the team members know what to focus on, what to do, or what to talk about? They won't. Without a clear purpose it is hard to know what is important and what can be ignored.

Years ago, I was working with an insurance company with about 125 employees. I was leading a training for the executive team, and we were talking about team purpose. I asked them, "What is your team's purpose?" They paused and looked around at each other.

Eventually, someone said, "Do you mean our mission statement?"

"No," I said. "Your mission statement is focused on the purpose of the entire organization. What is the purpose of this team? Why do you meet regularly? Why do you work together?"

After an awkward silence, the CEO made a sarcastic joke about how everyone was there to serve him.

We had work to do.

A clear team purpose helps you prioritize projects, manage your energy, and focus on what matters. It means you feel committed and work hard toward your goals.

When we are confused or do not have a clear direction, we stall. We do not make decisions. We often walk away and do nothing. The same thing happens for teams. If they are confused about their purpose, they wallow in indecision, they are not committed, and they are less focused. The lack of commitment and focus is mostly because of not knowing what they should be committed to.

Your team must be clear on its purpose and feel a sense of connection to it. That clarity and connection will lead to greater commitment. In my work, I have found that most people care deeply about the quality of their work and want to contribute to the world, no matter how big or small that contribution may be. Often a lack of commitment signals a lack of clarity. Teammates may not understand the team's purpose, or it may not resonate with them. There might not be clear goals, or no one is tracking progress toward the goals. In chapter 4, we will dive deeper into the unique nuances within team purpose that foster innovation.

Team Dynamics

Team dynamics are the behavior and interactions within a team and the relationships between the team members. Team dynamics influence a team's ability to be creative. Creativity requires risk. If team members do not have strong team dynamics with each other, they will not take the risks needed to be more creative together.

Specifically, the variables with the greatest impact on team creativity are trust, communication, and creative abrasion. Creative abrasion is a particular type of conflict where team members can disagree about the ideas and the work they are doing together, but they do not disagree because of personality or identity. They exhibit a level of grace and compassion when it comes to differing, even conflicting, personalities.

In chapter 5 we will go into more depth on team dynamics and you will gain a deeper understanding on the nuances of increasing trust, communication, and creative abrasion.

Team Creative Process

Many teams are familiar with the importance of developing a clear team purpose and cultivating strong team dynamics, but fewer understand the importance of knowing and using a team creative process. Team creative process is the team's use of the tools, techniques, and strategies needed to be creative. This includes the structure of team meetings, the way the agenda is designed, and how problems are presented and approached.

Team creative process is the crux of the Deliberate Creative Team system. Without a clear, shared process, the team will not advance to the sustainable or scalable levels of a Deliberate Creative Team.

How a group approaches a problem matters. Teams within highly creative organizations, such as Pixar Animation Studios or the product design company IDEO, use specific processes to develop new products.[13] The processes provide structure and methodology for a team's approach to tasks. Methodology affects a team's creativity.[14] Processes include the series of operations, actions, meeting norms, tools, and techniques, as well as the spirit of their approach and reflective practices.[15] Many creative processes are out there already, including creative problem solving, design thinking, human-centered design, TRIZ, and more. They are all similar. Picking one system (or a combination) and being sure every team member is trained in the process and knows how to use it are more important than which system you use. Then you need to implement the process in team meetings and projects. We will go into more depth on team creative process in chapter 6 and beyond.

THE DELIBERATE CREATIVE TEAM system provides a powerful framework for teams to be creative and innovate anytime. I will warn you, though—it is simple, but it is not easy. Leading a team through the changes it may need to become a Deliberate Creative Team at the sustainable or scalable level takes guts, conviction, and focus. There may be resistance from within the team and outside the team. But once you start producing results, the smiles will spread wider, the impact will build, and the revenue will grow.

But before we dig deeper into each of the three areas of Deliberate Creative Teams, we need to talk a bit more about teams.

3

The Source of Innovation in Organizations

OW MANY TEAMS have you been on in your life? Think about work teams, committees, volunteer teams, and sports teams—your family might even count. For me, there have been dozens, at least. Some were for a short time, others for a long time. Every job I have had, I have been on a team of some sort.

It makes sense that teams are such a big part of our lives. Teams allow multiple perspectives, skills, and expertise to come together and meld brainpower to achieve powerful results. Most significant projects, plans, and goals are too large and multifaceted for an individual to approach alone. Therefore, teams have become the quintessential unit of high performance.[1] Consequently, teams are one of the primary sources of creativity and innovation in organizations.[2]

Look around you. Notice all the inventions and designs humans have created. You might notice a faucet and the plumbing system it is connected to, the internet router and the worldwide connection it provides, your smartphone, computer, monitor, TV, coffee maker, chairs, and tables. Now, imagine the teams it took to create any of these items. Think beyond that one individual item, like the faucet, to the centuries of innovation required to get a beautiful stainless steel faucet to produce hot or cold water instantly with almost no effort on our part. It is phenomenal. Now, imagine we did not have teams. Imagine if the only innovations in our world were based on individual skills. I would not be writing a book on a computer right now. Planes, cars, computers, city-wide infrastructure, farming practices, even language would not exist. If you think about human civilization without collaboration, the image is staggering. Teams have made our world what it is today. They are critical for continued innovation. They have become even more important as our world has grown more complex.

Multiple studies have observed a trend toward collaborative research and innovation in recent years. In an analysis of 2.1 million patents and 1.9 million research papers over five decades, the research created by teams has increased significantly compared with research by individuals.[3] This holds true for all domains, including science, engineering, social sciences, humanities, and the arts. The way we work has evolved. The more complex our world is, the more critical teams are for innovation. Teams tend to generate more innovative ideas than individuals do. Team members bring diverse perspectives and expertise to address challenges.

In the research that led to his book *Creativity*, Dr. Mihaly Csikszentmihalyi studied nearly one hundred highly creative individuals to learn more about the trends and commonalities of highly creative people. The research participants included winners of Nobel Prizes and other top awards in their respective fields. They have significantly impacted the arts, sciences, and humanities around the world. During the extensive interviews, many participants recounted the importance of others in their creative process.[4]

Since Csikszentmihalyi's book was published in 1996, the research on creativity and teams has increased significantly, leading to a greater understanding of the nuances involved in creative teams. The research is unwavering: Creative teams are not the "simple sum of individual creative skills."[5] Teams have an incredible ability to solve huge, complex problems, but only if team members work well together. That is the kicker. A truly high-performing, innovative team is rare, but it does not have to be.

From Cooperation to Collaboration

Many years ago, when I was much less experienced, another consultant hired me to collaborate with him to develop a new team for a law school client of his. The school wanted its administrative assistants, who were working in various departments, to form a team. My job was to kick off the initiative by bringing the group together. I flew across the country to lead a day of team building. It was a small disaster.

Perhaps the initiative was the school's attempt to decrease silos throughout the campus, but there was massive resistance from the admin assistants because they insisted they were not a team. They repeatedly explained to my colleague and me, and the administration, that it did not make sense to call them a team because they did not and could not collaborate. Each department operated separately, and each admin assistant had individual work to complete. Sure, they could swap advice or support each other, but they had to do their own work.

At the time, I did not have a clear definition of the word "team." I had used it a zillion times in my life, but never truly thought about its definition. Shortly after that experience, I read the book *The Wisdom of Teams* by organizational consultants Jon R. Katzenbach and Douglas K. Smith. I realized

Teams have made our world what it is today. They are vital for continued innovation.

that the admin assistants were right. They were not a team and were not going to become one because their work did not fit with what a team is. Katzenbach and Smith's definition of teams is aspirational and instructive: "A team is a small number of people with complementary skills who are committed to a common purpose, performance goals, and approach for which they hold themselves mutually accountable."[6]

Instead, this group of admin assistants was what Katzenbach and Smith called a "working group." In a working group, "members interact primarily to share information, best practices, or perspectives and to make decisions to help each individual perform within his or her area of responsibility."[7]

I wish I had understood these definitions then because it would have shifted the work I did, and I could have been more effective. The admin assistants did not have a common purpose, goals, or approach and they were not collectively accountable for their work. Although they were all aligned with the bigger purpose of the school, they supported different departments, and their work was not interwoven.

I like Katzenbach and Smith's definition of a team because if a team is truly meeting all its criteria, it is going to be impressive. Teams working at this level can produce highly creative results that can positively affect their organizations, communities, or even the world. Think about teams that launch space shuttles at NASA, win the FIFA World Cup, design new tech products, or launch an award-winning local restaurant.

Working well toward a shared goal is not the same as getting along. Many teams I have consulted with get along well. Teammates enjoy each other's company and respect each other's work. It seems like they work well together. But when I ask more questions about their work or observe them in a meeting, I soon realize they are cooperative, but not collaborative.

The difference between cooperation and collaboration is critical. Cooperation is when team members support each other, share ideas, and have mutual respect; but they are, in the end, working independently and results are evaluated independently. Much like the admin assistants at the law school.

Collaboration is what Katzenbach and Smith are talking about. There is mutual accountability and trust. Team members become interdependent. They work together to produce something new. They move from sharing ideas to generating new ideas together. This work is deeper than cooperation. When I have had opportunities for true collaboration, I felt like I was in this amazing upward spiral where the work was fun and I lost track of time. We entered a state of group flow and were in the zone. When teams can truly collaborate, they can be creative together.

When I think back to my experience with Phil and the university team that I mentioned in chapter 2, I now have a much better sense of what was going on. We were highly cooperative. We were nice to each other. We got along well, for the most part. We enjoyed each other's company. We supported each other when needed. Occasionally, we were even collaborative, but mostly we were just cooperative.

Our failed brainstorming session was not Phil's fault. We were never going to be creative together because we did not understand how creativity worked and did not have a system for being creative together. Like most teams, we showed up to regular meetings. We thought we were doing great because we had an agenda each week. We enjoyed the occasional team-building experience or excursion. We laughed and joked with each other. But we did not work on ourselves as a team. It all felt surface-level. Our leader was not particularly vulnerable, and therefore, we were not willing to be vulnerable about our flaws and strengths. We were not serious about our performance, not collectively willing to do the deep work. I still feel a sense of loss about that team because we had incredible potential, but we just could not quite figure out how to maximize our collective strength. I now realize this lack of true collaboration is far too common.

There is a beautiful film called *Where There Once Was Water*, directed by photographer Brittany App. Through App's stunning videography, the film explains the massive water crisis in the United States and the world. Water is a precious resource that we have mismanaged for decades, and now we are in serious trouble.[8] I live in an area of the country where it rains frequently and water is abundant. I am not that knowledgeable about the water issues in California and elsewhere.

When the film ended I watched the credits roll with a furrowed brow. I was surprised to learn that we have plenty of solutions. The technology, skills, and knowledge to solve the problem sustainably already exist. The good news is that we do not need another dam that will drown our sacred spaces. We do not need to divert another river. People have already invented brilliant, creative solutions to address water scarcity. The limitation is our ability to collaborate. The skills of collaboration and creativity are critical. Without those skills, we miss out on solving big problems with novel, viable solutions.

By now, you understand what creativity is, that there is a Deliberate Creative Team system, and the importance of teams. If you are ready to get serious about deliberate creativity in your teams, let's look in more depth at the system and what you need to lead a Deliberate Creative Team that can innovate anytime. I will give you the strategies and tools you need to clarify team purpose, develop strong team dynamics, and understand and use the team creative process you need. You will be able to truly collaborate and innovate on demand. Let's start with team purpose.

Activity: Make a Team Toolbox

Purpose: to put together the supplies you need to facilitate various creative processes during your team meetings

Time: fifteen to sixty minutes

Materials: varies, see below

An easy step you can take as you start systematizing creativity into your team's work is to have all the supplies you need on hand. I suggest making a simple team toolbox and bringing it to each meeting. Having a box of supplies ready to go will help you respond in the moment with the best tool or technique. Several activities in this book use the supplies listed here.

For in-person meetings, I recommend:

- Standard size (3″ x 3″) sticky notes in assorted colors, enough so that each person can have a pad
- Additional sticky notes in different sizes, such as 3″ x 5″ (larger) or 2″ x 2″ (smaller)
- Dark pens or thin markers for writing on sticky notes
- Notecards
- Scrap paper
- Little sticker dots for voting on the best ideas
- Flipcharts or dry-erase boards
- Markers for flipcharts or dry-erase boards
- Facilitation cards such as Climer Cards (more on these shortly)
- Fidget toys or pipe cleaners to play with
- A box that fits all the supplies and is easy to transport to each meeting

Bring your box of supplies to every meeting. Place it in the middle of the table or another prominent location so that anyone can access the supplies and initiate an activity using the tools. You might not use it for three meetings in a row, but keep bringing the box. (To see an example of a creative meetings toolbox, visit climerconsulting.com/extras.)

For virtual meetings, your supplies need to be digital, not physical. While you might suggest that everyone have scrap paper and fidget toys available, you also need to use online-based collaborative tools. This takes a little more effort than just putting together a box of props, but the results are worth it. I suggest the following.

Mural or Miro. These tools are brilliant for collaborating online. In an online space, they mimic a whiteboard and allow groups to use sticky notes, voting dots, et cetera. The learning curve may be a bit longer than with some software (meaning it likely takes fifteen minutes rather than two minutes to learn). If you are willing to take the time to learn it, the tools will revolutionize how you work and your creative results. I use Mural when I lead longer virtual trainings or facilitations with my clients. They love it.

Video conferencing tools. How well do you and your team members know platforms like Zoom, Microsoft Teams, and so on? Is your knowledge limited to the mute button and screen sharing? If so, spend time learning the other features and use them. Zoom has a built-in whiteboard, annotation tools, and many more features that can help you have a better meeting. Taking fifteen minutes to learn them will help you lead better creative meetings virtually.

Climer Cards platform. Climer Cards are a simple deck of cards that allow facilitators to combine visual images and metaphors to deepen conversations and connections. In addition to physical decks, Climer Cards exist on a robust virtual platform. There are multiple decks in the platform, and you can even upload your own deck. (Learn more at climercards.com/virtual.)

Climer Cards: Learn more at **climercards.com**.

The Clarifying Force of Team Purpose

THROUGHOUT MY TWENTIES and thirties, I was always on a soccer team—indoor, outdoor, co-ed, or women's—all combinations. At first glance, you might think that the purpose of a sports team is to win games, but not necessarily. I learned this early on in my twenties when I joined a co-ed team in Portland, Oregon. I had just moved to the city and was looking for new friends and a soccer team. I went to the local indoor soccer facility and saw a hand-scrawled note on the bulletin board: "Looking for female players for Sunday night co-ed team. Call Doug." I called.

Doug asked me some questions about my experience and then said, "It sounds like you have the experience level that would fit well with our team, but perhaps the most important question is, do you like to drink beer?" I laughed and said yes.

Doug did not care whether I drank beer, but he wanted to know if I was the type of person who would enjoy hanging out with the team after the game. That is what they cared about. They liked to win, but more than that they liked connecting and enjoying one another's company. The team's purpose was clear from day one, and I was all in.

That team was the best team I have been on in over twenty years of playing soccer. I was twenty-three years old and the youngest player. Our oldest player was Ginger, who was sixty-seven. She was not fast, but she was a solid defender who knew the game well. We had strong players, we cared about each other, and we passed to each other. A common problem in recreational co-ed soccer is that stronger, faster men get the ball and do not pass it to the women, essentially ignoring half their teammates. The entire team suffers because you cannot be effective with only half a team. But this team was different. If a man on our team acted like that, he was called out. If it continued, Doug asked him to find another team. The purpose of the team was clear. It was not a place for showboating or winning at all costs. This group had a deep love for the game and each other. Of course, a nice side effect of all this camaraderie was that we did win lots of games and more than once were the league champion.

I do not always love sports examples because they can oversimplify teams in the workplace, whose situations are different from sports teams. I believe in this case it works. With a clear purpose, we were aligned in our vision and met our purpose: having fun and playing good soccer.

A purpose does not have to be complicated.

Study after study has shown that teams with a shared purpose outperform those who are less clear. Without a clear, shared purpose, there is little output. What is the point of your team? Why do you meet regularly? How do you know what to focus on?

The role of a team is to collectively work toward a shared purpose. "Purpose" may also refer to vision, mission, legacy, dream, goal, performance results, or calling. This need for a shared purpose applies to sports teams, work teams, and your trivia team that meets Wednesday night at the local pub. In each case the purpose is different, but they all have (or should have) a shared purpose. However, in many cases, there is no discussion of it. Perhaps the team leader has a general idea, but it may not be clear to all the team members. When team members are clear on the purpose, they can adjust their approach to best meet that purpose and therefore produce better results for the team.

The Power of Team Purpose

In the 1980s, Jeffrey K. Pinto from the University of Cincinnati and John E. Prescott from the University of Pittsburgh were curious about the factors that impact the success of a project throughout its life.[1] While many variables impact a team, was everything of equal weight? What about for different stages of the project? Would the important variables change at each stage?

Pinto and Prescott surveyed 418 project managers and asked them about current projects, specifically inquiring about which variables mattered at each stage. Each manager focused on one project, identified which stage it was in, and answered questions so the researchers could determine which variables were positively impacting the project. The results showed that only one variable was critical for every stage. That was purpose. A clear, shared purpose is critical across all stages of a project, whether or not you are trying to be creative. And if innovation is the top priority? Purpose still matters.

Fifteen years later, Craig Pearce from the Peter F. Drucker Graduate School of Management, Claremont Graduate University, and Michael Ensley from Rensselaer Polytechnic

Institute were curious about the connection between a team's shared vision and their level of innovation. They studied seventy-one teams at a US automotive plant that made transmissions and engines.[2]

Several years earlier the company had experienced severe labor-management disputes, which resulted in three bomb threats and a murder-suicide attempt. The work environment was poor, to say the least. In response, the company shifted its focus to a more collaborative, team-based approach. It invited one of the researchers to consult on their innovation process.

Each of the seventy-one teams was charged with product or process innovation that focused on areas like component design and development, engineering change control and administrative systems, and manufacturing systems. The team managers, internal customers, and team members were surveyed twice: once when the team was forming and several months later as the projects were finishing. The results showed that those teams that had a clearer vision at the beginning developed more innovative results and that the innovative results reciprocally reinforced the vision, increasing its clarity. This positive loop meant that team members stayed focused and motivated while their creativity also increased.

Team purpose is the group's collective focus. It also encompasses shared goals and the team's commitment to reaching the goals. Without commitment, goals are just a list of targets that a team does not *share* responsibility for. And commitment is not possible without shared goals, because what would the team be committing to? Whether a team meets its goals or not can be due, in part, to whether team members feel the goals are clear and the project is aligned with the team's purpose.

For example, imagine you are part of a learning and development department. A recent company survey identified that new employees are not feeling welcomed into the organization. The executive team decides that changing this is a top priority. You agree. Your team is asked to redesign the onboarding process so that new employees feel included and connected to the organization's mission, values, and culture. Your team's purpose is to "cultivate a culture of continuous improvement by developing top-notch learning programs that provide all employees with the tools to contribute to the organization's strategic goals."

Your team discusses the assignment and how it fits with your purpose. They agree there is direct alignment, and they feel energized about the new program. They start by developing a list of goals that looks something like this:

- Schedule next meeting
- Research onboarding
- Interview employees
- Talk with employees who quit
- Metrics

But at the next meeting, most team members have not finished their assigned tasks. They have been busy with other work and feel overwhelmed. Stress and apathy have replaced the initial energy about the project. What if that stress and apathy are caused by a lack of clarity around the goals? Team members may not be sure what they are committing to. The conversation around the goals might have felt clear in the moment, but a week later when, for example, the person leading the goal called "metrics" relooks at it, they cannot remember exactly what that means. They tell themselves to ask another team member, but then get distracted by an email and do not do it. The tasks weigh on them, and they feel worried that they are not getting the work done.

If the team also did not have a clear team purpose, team members might even ask, "Are we sure this is in our purview and not HR's?" That lack of clarity may further degrade commitment and stagnate action.

On the other hand, what if the goals were clear and even inspiring? We'll talk more about shared goals later in this chapter, but for the purposes of this example, a few of your team's shared goals might look like this:

- Schedule two hours to apply the creative process to the challenge.

- Research what other companies do to onboard their employees. Look for unique ideas and identify examples of best practices.

- Interview three to five recent hires and find out what they wish their onboarding process had been like.

- Interview at least three people who left the company in the last year. Find out what they wished their onboarding process had been like.

- Determine what metric to use to measure the success of the new onboarding program.

You divide the tasks up among team members and set deadlines for each. Now the goals feel clear and aligned with the team's purpose.

Developing a clear team purpose and writing clear goals and tasks every time are simple ways to enact this principle. Simple does not mean easy, though. Many teams have never discussed their team purpose. Often when I ask teams to tell me their team purpose, teammates mumble and fumble and cannot answer the question.

How about your team? Have you talked about your purpose? If so, how recently? I recommend at least once per year and regularly referencing it throughout the year so it stays fresh in everyone's minds.

Team purpose is the group's collective focus, its shared goals, and its commitment to reaching the goals.

You Must Be Clear

For a team to be clear on its shared purpose, the leader needs to be clear. This may seem obvious, but it does not always happen. Here is an example. Through my consulting practice, I was hired by a large university to assist in reorganizing one department with about seventy-five employees. I was charged with guiding three new teams through the restructuring process. The team members were dedicated, motivated, and eager to do well in their new team. Even though the process of change was difficult, they believed the changes were positive and would be valuable in the long run. Because of the transition, some team members were temporarily doing two jobs and everyone was overwhelmed with the volume of work.

The team members did not feel they had the authority to determine the priorities within their work, so they sought the input of their supervisor, a member of the executive team. When they asked him how to best prioritize, he was vague and said everything was important. This caused more frustration and stress. They asked me to please talk with him. I explained to him what was going on, that their confusion was leading to stress and decreasing their motivation and commitment. He still would not prioritize the work. I soon realized it was not that he was being obstinate or unwilling. He just did not know. He did not have a clear sense of purpose, and he could not figure out the priorities. Knowing the purpose allows us to prioritize goals and guides us in determining what is important and what is not.

With this new information, the teammates realized they were on their own. We sequestered ourselves in a conference room for a few hours and mapped out the goals and tasks on the walls. We were eventually able to develop a clear purpose and prioritize. It took a half day, but the resulting motivation and focus they felt made every minute worthwhile.

For teams, sometimes a clear purpose comes from supervisors or others who are higher up. Sometimes you need to go forth with minimal guidance and figure it out among yourselves. Whichever the approach, be careful to not throw up your hands when you do not get a clear answer from above. Take the time to work through it together.

On one hand, team purpose seems like such a simple concept, but when faced with the complexities of organizational life, it can be a challenge for a team to narrow in on one purpose. After that half day where we clarified the purpose and goals, the team could move forward with more energy and ease. They knew what to focus on and when. It made the department reorganization more efficient and effective. With a clear sense of purpose, prioritization becomes evident, shared goals are easier to create and follow, and team commitment soars.

The following is an activity that will clarify your team's purpose.

Activity: Talk about Team Purpose

Purpose: to clarify the team's purpose and ensure each team member understands it

Time: fifteen to thirty minutes

Materials: index cards or sticky notes, at least one per person

To start, pass out an index card, sticky note, or piece of scrap paper to each person. Ask each person to quietly write down what they see as the team's purpose. This should be one to two sentences.

After everyone has finished, place the cards in the middle of the table or post them on the wall. Gather around and ask each person to read a card out loud. Then spend time comparing and sorting the responses. Is there a clear alignment on the purpose? Or are the responses unclear or different from each other?

If there is alignment, see if the team can easily craft a one- to two-sentence purpose that resonates with everyone. This is not a vision statement that will be engraved on the wall. You do not need to get deep into the weeds of wordsmithing. The goal is to have something short that everyone agrees on. Ide- ally, each team member should be able to explain the purpose in less than one minute.

On the other hand, if the responses on the cards seem vague, unclear, or diverse, spend time exploring a common purpose. This will be a longer conversation and may require additional, separate time. Please do not skimp on this. The activity is not just about getting a clear purpose statement. The process of the conversation is important. You want team members to be heard and feel they played a role in developing the purpose. Sure, the team leader could just write something up and hand it out, but it has less value if it is just handed down from above. The conversation aids team members in connecting to the purpose and to each other. This increases commitment and team performance.

For most of us, our memory is not great. It is easy for a team to forget that purpose. Bring up the purpose regularly. It should be reflected in your decisions, your emails, and your conversations about projects. Be repetitive. Be redundant. Be congruent. Always connect the work back to the purpose.

From Shared Purpose to Shared Goals

Sometimes teams have a clear, shared purpose, but they stop there. Without creating goals, the purpose may feel nebulous or wishful. Goals are how we know we are getting to the purpose. Goals are especially valuable in a creative team because they provide a way to communicate with each other and ensure alignment.

I have worked with hundreds of teams as a consultant. A few years ago I asked one team how they tracked their goals along with the tasks related to reaching each goal. They looked at me like I had two heads. They had no idea what I was talking about. Since then I have been asking this question to many teams and leaders. Over half do not collectively track tasks or goals.

Shared goals only count if they are written down. Team members are not going to remember them. We have too many other things in our heads. Again, you are human; your memory is fallible. Make teamwork easier by writing down tasks and goals. Develop your goals as a team, and then make them visual with a spreadsheet or project management software, at the top of each meeting agenda, or on the whiteboard in the work area. Pick what fits your team's style.

Let's imagine that you are in a team meeting discussing a particular project your team is working on. At the end of the meeting, at least half of the team members have written down specific tasks they need to complete. Individually, they add them to their to-do lists. Great!

The following week at another meeting about the same project, you are checking in to see how the team is progressing toward their goals. You can ask each person to report on their accomplishments, but this is time-consuming. Plus, what if someone forgot their task? If you have ten smart people in a room for one hour, giving bland updates on task accomplishment does not sound like a good use of time. It is draining and boring, and it does not lead to collaboration or team commitment. Use those team meetings to work through issues and challenges. Make use of that collective, creative brainpower. You are striving for innovation, not compliance.

What if, instead, you could just pull up a spreadsheet or task management software that each person updated in advance? In less than a minute, you can see who has finished which tasks and what remains. This will shift the conversation and the collective energy. Now you can talk about what is getting in the way, bottlenecks that have arisen, unexpected problems, and you can celebrate successes. This is a better use of those powerful brains in the meeting. It also leads to creative ideas, new approaches, and true innovation. If your team meetings are boring, you might be doing it wrong. We will talk more about team meetings in later chapters.

For now, you can start to ensure you have shared goals with the following activity.

Activity: Record the Team's Goals and Tasks

Purpose: to create a visual record of shared team goals

Time: fifteen minutes to two hours

Materials: blank paper, sticky notes, a shared document, and/or task management software

Invite team members to work together and list the team's goals. To start, jot down the goals in any order. If you are using sticky notes, put one goal on each sticky note. If you are in a spreadsheet, one per row. Adjust according to your materials.

One person can be a scribe or, my preference, everyone can write or add to the spreadsheet at the same time. It might be a little messy, but it saves time and engages everyone.

Then do a quick scan to make sure you have all the goals and they are written in a clear way that everyone understands. Start each goal with an action verb, such as "develop," "design," "create," "make," or "file." The way you write the goal impacts what you focus on. Recall the examples from earlier in the chapter:

- A poorly written goal/task: Metrics.

- A well-written goal/task: Determine what metric we will use to measure success of our new onboarding program.

"Metrics" is not a goal. It is a noun. When you look at it a month later and read "metrics," it is difficult to remember what you were talking about. This confusion creates inaction. The clarity you get from easy-to-understand tasks and goals will lead to more action, more progress, and therefore more innovation.

When you start writing goals with more clarity, it may feel awkward, but over time it will get easier and come more naturally. You are building a skill, a muscle. It is like learning to do a pull-up. You start by blindly kicking the air with a painful grimace and lots of grunts. Soon you get smoother and eventually ten reps feel easy. Nothing to it, right?

A Cycle of Purpose, Goals, and Commitment

Once you have clarified your team purpose and recorded your team goals, your team will work on developing its commitment. The collective sense of purpose can unite a team and bring about great commitment. Team commitment can be defined

A collective
sense of purpose
can unite a
team **and bring
about great
commitment.**

as "the relative strength of an individual's identification with and involvement in a particular team."[3] There are three characteristics of team commitment:

- A strong belief in and acceptance of the team's values and goals

- A desire to work hard on behalf of the team

- A strong desire to remain a team member[4]

There are many stories of people sacrificing significantly to give to a team. For instance, in the book *Creativity, Inc.*, cofounder of Pixar Animation Studios Ed Catmull talks about the tremendous commitment team members exhibited in the creation of the movie *Toy Story 2*. The team worked up to one hundred hours a week and sacrificed emotional and physical health to reach the vision of creating a cutting-edge, innovative film. While this level of commitment is extreme and unhealthy (and even Catmull spoke to the dangers of the intensity of the work), it nevertheless demonstrates the impact of commitment. Team members had a clear sense of purpose, shared goals, and a strong commitment, leading to high levels of innovation. *Toy Story 2* was heralded as "one of the only sequels to ever outshine the original"[5] and would eventually top $500 million at the box office.

Lee Unkrich, who worked on the film, said, "We had done the impossible. We had done the thing that everyone told us we couldn't do. And we had done it spectacularly well. It was the fuel that has continued to burn in all of us."[6]

In a study of the effectiveness of seventy-five high-performing teams, researchers and consultants Carl Larson and Frank LaFasto interviewed leaders and members of impressive management and project teams across a range of industries, from organizations such as NASA, the White House, and the National Football League. They found that a unified commitment to the team was one of the commonalities among successful teams. The commitment came in the form of team spirit, dedication and loyalty, excitement and enthusiasm, and most of all a strong identification with the team and a willingness to work hard to succeed. The authors pointed out the importance of balancing individuality and team commitment. Too much team commitment leads to groupthink, whereas too little leads to analysis paralysis as the team attempts to sort out the competing needs.[7]

Sometimes Purpose Isn't First

Despite everything I have just described about the importance of a shared purpose to drive innovation, there is an exception. In 2018, Johnathan Cromwell published a study arguing that there are times when purpose comes later, not at the beginning.[8] Cromwell studied a start-up company that was creating a social robot. He explained that a social robot is a device "designed to interact with humans through verbal communication while exhibiting some type of emotional or social intelligence." The company had a loose vision to create a social robot for the home. They did not know the purpose of the robot or what it would do. They only knew it would be a robot designed to help people. Their specific problem was ill-defined. They were not trying to create a robot for a certain task, but rather to see what they could develop and then find a need for it.

When the concept and need are ambiguous, the innovation process becomes more iterative, and its purpose evolves through incremental clarification. This is more common in situations of breakthrough innovation such as when new technology is being developed or possible resources do not yet exist.

This is how Post-its were invented—and thank goodness they were. I love Post-its! In 1968, Spencer Silver, a chemist at 3M, was trying to make a highly potent adhesive for airplanes. Instead, he developed a low-tack adhesive called acrylate copolymer microsphere that did not have an immediate use. He patented it in 1972. Two years later, Arthur Fry, a chemical engineer also at 3M, heard a lecture by Silver promoting the adhesive. He tried the adhesive to prevent a small problem he had with paper bookmarks falling out of his hymnal when he sang at church. By 1980, Post-it Notes were available throughout the United States, and in 1993 Fry applied for the patent.

In certain situations, the emergent innovation process of identifying a purpose after a solution is ideal, but it also may be more time-consuming. In the case of the social robot, during the three years it took the company to develop and release the robot, technology advanced rapidly, and other social robots were being created. One year after its release, the company sold its assets and shut down. The Post-it Note was also years in the making because it took time to find a useful solution that would stick. (Pun intended.)

In both of these examples, there was still a purpose, although a loose one. For the Post-its, it was to figure out how the adhesive might be used. For the social robot, they knew they wanted to make a social robot for homes. Those two purposes guided the creative process as the inventors generated and tested new ideas, but ultimately the purpose for the end product was evolving. This approach, in which the innovation guides the purpose, tends to be slower, but the results can be more groundbreaking.

In most situations, a team should develop a clear purpose from the beginning with the caveat that it can evolve if needed. A clear purpose gives you something to check against regularly. You can ask yourselves, Does this new idea align with our focus? However, since you are trying to be creative, be careful about a purpose that is too narrow. Innovation is about creating something new, and if the purpose is too tight, it may restrict you.

That said, teams can choose either a looser team purpose to allow more divergent ideas or a tighter one. It depends a lot on your type of team, your circumstances, and how innovative you want to be. There is no right or wrong here. What is important is that your team talks about its purpose and is aligned with it. A clear team purpose will drive their motivation, deepen commitment, and improve your results.

5

The Key Ingredients in Team Dynamics

EVERAL YEARS into my consulting practice, I was recruited by a small but mighty organization to facilitate leadership trainings for government executives. I joined a team of seasoned, smart, skilled facilitators who designed and delivered meaningful leadership programs. A few of us lived in another state and had to join team meetings remotely via phone. (This was a few years before the COVID pandemic, so Zoom and other platforms were not widespread yet.) A couple of months after I started, our team leader informed us we would all be reading a book together and using it as a guide to develop and improve our team. I had already read the book and thought this was a great idea. Most of the team members had been around for years, so I was eager to dig into the topics together and deepen my connections with them.

At the next meeting, as we were discussing the book, another team member posed a question about developing trust, and I shared an idea in response. As soon as I finished sharing the idea, she snapped at me, saying my comments had nothing to do with her question. I was flummoxed by her strong reaction. It seems I misunderstood the question. I thought that maybe without the benefit of seeing her body language or knowing the team's history, I missed a nuance. I waited for clarification, but none came. If this had happened earlier in my career, it would have rocked me. Instead, I just shook my head and decided to be quieter at future team meetings.

I also started thinking about team dynamics. Where was the grace? Why had she been so abrasive when I misunderstood her? What was the history of this group, and why were the team dynamics subpar? This was a highly intelligent group and most of the team members had some background in leadership or team development. Go figure.

I did not stay in that position long. It was an intermittent, part-time role, and I had been recruited to join the team while I was also leading my consulting practice. After a few experiences like the one above, I could feel myself pulling away from the group. I dreaded the team meetings. I liked the work with the clients, but I was not interested in being part of a team with poor team dynamics. I also was not in a situation where I could have much influence on the group. Had there been a strong sense of community based on trust, I would have stayed because the work would have been rewarding and fun.

Small comments like the one above quickly erode trust. That moment taught me that if I did share in this group, I had better be right or risk a scolding. I do not last long in groups like that. My motivation fades, I check out, and I know there are better opportunities, full of trust, elsewhere. In retrospect, I can see that the team dynamics led me toward quiet quitting, something I am not proud of. According to Gallup and the *Harvard Business Review*, quiet quitting is when employees do the minimum amount of work and do not go above and beyond.[1] One contributing factor may be poor team dynamics.

Fortunately, many times I have also had the opposite experience, where I was part of a team with excellent team dynamics.

If you want your team to be creative together, they need to work well together. I know, it seems obvious. But obvious does not mean easy. Of the three elements teams need to be creative together (team purpose, team dynamics, and team creative process), team dynamics is the hardest and most complex, but the results are worth the work.

Team dynamics are the behaviors and interactions within a team and the relationships between the team members. These competencies are not to be taken lightly. Strong team dynamics require emotional intelligence, empathy, and vulnerability to get to moderate or high levels of trust, communication, and creative abrasion. Let's probe further into each of these and how they impact a team.

An Environment of Trust

Trust is a tough thing. It takes time to build, although it can happen faster than you might think. It can also be lost quickly, sometimes in just one moment. This makes trust somewhat precious. Trust and its close cousin psychological safety are necessary if you want to have strong communication and for the team to engage in creative abrasion. Trust and psychological safety are critical to any team, but especially for one trying to be creative together. You must create a culture where team members can share their ideas without fear of retribution or being knocked down. Before going further, let's examine the differences between trust and psychological safety, because they are subtle but significant.

Psychological safety, sometimes called participative safety or group trust, is where team members feel emotionally safe to share their ideas, perceptions, and opinions. The environment is interpersonally nonthreatening, and team members are motivated to be involved in decision-making. The difference between trust and psychological safety is that trust is focused more on individual relationships, whereas psychological safety is focused more on the full team. Teams with higher levels of trust and psychological safety can engage in the real work needed to be creative together and produce innovative results. The key to building trust is creating an environment with a high level of psychological safety.

Being creative means sharing ideas, trying something new, and taking risks together. This will never happen without at least a moderate level of psychological safety within your team. Think about colleagues you trust compared to those you do not trust. You are more likely to share a wacky idea or be candid with your opinions with someone you trust. Trust creates the space for healthy disagreement and debate about ideas. You feel more relaxed and free to be yourself. You are not guarded and do not measure your words carefully. Trust and psychological safety are the foundation of true collaboration.

Years ago, an insurance company hired me to teach their mid-level managers leadership skills. I designed a program for them based on their core principles. The work went well, and soon the vice president of organizational development asked me to lead a few sessions with their executive team so they could work better together.

During one of our sessions, I led an exercise designed to build trust and psychological safety within the group. Each person developed a list of responses to the phrase "If you really knew me, you would know" and then shared out loud. As we sat in a circle, the team was fully present and vulnerable. One team member shared that she had cancer and had been going through chemotherapy for several months. Only

Being creative means trying something new and taking risks together. **This will not happen without psychological safety within your team.**

one other team member knew this. I was surprised that she was dealing with such a huge life change and her colleagues did not know.

Others shared about loss and love or challenges they had faced. Tissues were passed around. There was a deep sense of compassion and care in the room. The feeling of connection was vibrant. My heart was full.

And then it was the CEO's turn.

The CEO shared some trite, surface-level details about his favorite food and that he had two siblings. His tone was flat, and he seemed to be put off by the whole experience. I encouraged him to share a bit more, and he refused. He was aloof, detached, and disinterested.

The rest of the team had chosen to be open and vulnerable, so I was appalled by his reaction. His decision highlighted the source of the team's problem and eroded the team's trust and sense of psychological safety even further. My heart sank.

Harvard professor Amy Edmondson has written extensively and done several studies on psychological safety.[2] Edmondson and other researchers point out that one of the most effective ways leaders can build psychological safety is by modeling vulnerability. Leaders do not need to share their deepest concerns or most private thoughts, but they need to show some humanity. Share a bit with colleagues. Trusting someone we do not know can be difficult. In the situation above, the CEO had a prime opportunity to open up and be human. Instead, he made it clear he would not be vulnerable nor would he support vulnerability within his most important team.

I knew that, unless he did some deep work, as long as he was leading this company the executive team would never truly have psychological safety or trust. Without that critical level of psychological safety, they would not share new ideas or engage in meaningful dialogue together. They would not be able to develop innovative solutions to their problems. They would continue to trudge along, maintaining the status quo, and that would prevent the entire company from being more innovative.

If anything, they were going to bond over his horrible leadership. But bonding against something is never as strong as bonding *for* something. The CEO needed serious coaching and probably therapy if he was going to be a better leader. Most likely he would not engage in either. Fortunately, he retired a few years later.

Team members need a culture where they are free to be themselves and bring their best selves to work. This means they are not worried about sarcastic comments or being bashed for their clothing choices, their weekend plans, their family of origin, their accent, or anything else. There is an environment of caring and, dare I say, love. Team members do not need to be best friends or hang out after work. They need to be able to be candid with each other about the work they do together.

If you are thinking this sounds hokey or too woo-woo, I suggest checking your own biases. Building a sense of psychological safety is anything but hokey. It takes a lot of work, and if you are feeling snideness toward the idea, you may be impeding your own or your team's ability to be deliberately creative.

As a leader, the way you show up and model vulnerability is critical. Are you creating an environment where you share who you truly are while also welcoming others? Or are you dismissive and threatened by vulnerability? Can team members share ideas without fear of being smacked down or ridiculed?

It may seem fluffy to worry about creating an environment that fosters a sense of inclusion and invites new ideas. But we are not robots. We are human. Like it or not, we are driven by emotion. This does not mean we are "emotional." It means that as rational as we would like to think we are, our feelings and intuition play a huge role in all areas of our lives. Teams must foster a sense of psychological safety to create an environment where creativity thrives. You can ignore the research at your peril or embrace it and learn to create a positive, supportive, and highly innovative space.

Different types of interpersonal trust are important for teams. Gloria Barczak, a professor at Northeastern University, and her team researched how trust impacts team creativity. She points out two types of trust.

Cognitive trust refers to "one's willingness to rely on a team member's expertise and reliability." It is when team members believe another member will do what they say they will do. It is closely related to integrity. The other type, affective trust, is "the confidence one places in a team member based on one's feelings of caring and concern illustrated by that co-worker."[3] It is sometimes called vulnerability-based trust. It is also the belief that I can be myself and bring my best self to the team. I know that my team members will not belittle me for an unworthy idea or unintelligent remark.

Numerous studies from 1976 to the present show that both cognitive and affective trust are important to a team's creative performance. When teams first form, cognitive trust is most important, but as teams mature, affective trust increases in relevance.

Think about a time when you were on a new team. During those initial meetings you were mentally scanning your teammates to determine if they could meet the performance expectations. You might not have been aware you were doing this, but it is a natural part of how we interact as humans. We want to know if our teammates have the knowledge, skills, and abilities to contribute to achieving our team's goals. If they do, we place a higher level of cognitive trust in them. We evaluate this based on tasks they complete, questions they ask, or contributions they make. This applies to an executive team, a software development team, a basketball team, or a Habitat for Humanity volunteer team.

As you start to understand their abilities, you move into analyzing their interpersonal behaviors. What are they like in team meetings? Are they supportive or does their sarcasm cause a rift? Do they listen or do they just want to share their own stories and perspectives? Again, this analysis may not be conscious on your part. Our brains automatically do this as a way to scan for threats and decide what is safe for us. When team members show a sense of caring and concern for each other, it creates a space that says, "We want you here. Please bring your full self and your best work." That leads to a positive environment that helps teams thrive at the highest levels.

The intersections of cognitive and affective trust can feel a bit complicated. If someone is not highly skilled, this does not mean they are "untrustworthy" in the way we typically use that word. The level of cognitive trust we place in someone is related to their skill level, but often how "trustworthy" they are is related to their awareness of their skills.

If someone peacocks around about their skills yet cannot deliver, it decreases your trust in them. But if someone is open and transparent that they are working on building their skills in a certain area, then that increases your trust in them. At this intersection of cognitive and affective trust, your assessment of their work-related skills relates to cognitive trust, but the way you feel about how they talk about their skills versus the reality of them is connected to affective trust.

For instance, let's say your team is presenting a proposal to an important client. You want the best sales presenter to lead—someone who is personable, makes quick connections,

**Team members
need a culture
where they are free**
to be themselves
and bring their best
selves to work.

is skilled in explaining the process, and feels comfortable with selling. You do not need the highest technical lead for the presentation. You want the person in whom you have the highest level of cognitive trust. There is a time and place for someone who is building their skills to lead a presentation. It just might not be this one.

When I have been in environments with high levels of both cognitive and affective trust, teammates could share ideas and perspectives and it strengthened our relationships. Teammates listened and responded positively. This does not mean they agreed. It meant they were open and willing to explore another angle, even if just for a moment.

Developing trust and psychological safety requires a fair bit of individual skill from each team member. In a research study by Google's Project Aristotle, the results showed that one of the skills team members needed for psychological safety is a high level of social sensitivity. This means they are proficient at perceiving and understanding others' feelings and perceptions, often based on tone of voice, body language, and other expressions.[4] Team members are aware of their own behavior and that of others. They are gauging if someone feels left out or snubbed. They are also quick to repair blunders. In the example above where my teammate rebuked me for misunderstanding her, or the example in chapter 2 where Phil shot down the idea and halted the brainstorming, there was little awareness on their part of the damage their actions were causing.

Please know, though, that I am not saying there is anything wrong with pointing out a misunderstanding or a flaw in an idea. In fact, please do. It would be worse to move forward with an idea and later learn that one teammate noticed something but did not speak up. That is the danger of groupthink. But speaking up against an idea is all about timing and style.

We will talk about when and how to criticize an idea in the next chapter when we talk about team creative process.

On Conflict, and Why You Need It

Years ago, I was teaching a two-day workshop on managing conflict to a group of professionals in Wisconsin. To kick off the workshop, I laid out a deck of Climer Cards on the table. I designed the deck with fifty-two watercolor paintings of subjects such as an elephant, an inchworm, a rotary telephone, a spool of thread, and a candle. The bright images spark new ideas, increase interactions, and deepen connection to content.

I asked each person to pick a Climer Card that represented their definition of conflict. Each person showed the group their card and explained their definition. The responses were all over the place. What one person viewed as conflict never even occurred to another. We were all fascinated. No wonder there is unnecessary tension in teams!

In creative teams, some conflict is needed because disagreements can lead to deeper thinking around creative challenges. But conflict can be challenging. It can be hard to know when to embrace conflict to help the team better solve a problem, or avoid it because the conflict signals an underlying issue that needs to be addressed. Fortunately, of all the internal dynamics within a team, conflict is the most studied.

Relationship Conflict versus Task Conflict

Teams may experience two types of conflict: relationship conflict and task conflict. Understanding the differences between these two can help team members engage in healthy conflict. Relationship conflict is when team members disagree with

Climer Cards: Learn more at **climercards.com**.

each other because of personality or identity (for example, race, gender, sexual orientation). Task conflict is when team members disagree about the work itself. This may include which idea to pursue, how to move forward with an idea, or if and how to gather more information.

Relationship conflict involves interpersonal incompatibilities among team members. Tension, animosity, annoyance, frustration, and anger between team members are all signs of relationship conflict. Relationship conflict distracts team members from their tasks and restricts their scope of attention. It does not aid any aspect of team performance, especially not innovation. Think about the times you have been engaged in a hallway conversation with someone complaining about another colleague's personality. That is relationship conflict. It is distracting from the real work. It is not helpful.

Relationship conflict leads to decreased satisfaction and increases the likelihood that team members will look for new jobs.[5] When team members experience chronic relationship conflict at work and they cannot figure out how to resolve it, they may disengage and look elsewhere.

Of course, sometimes relationship conflict happens, as this is a normal part of our human experience. The key is to address it in a healthy way that leads to shared understanding and mutual respect. Ignoring it or encouraging it is not helpful.

In creative teams, task conflict is welcomed because disagreements can lead to deeper thinking around creative challenges. A moderate amount of task conflict highlights different perspectives and can unearth potential problems and issues that if explored early can be avoided or mitigated. Moderation is the key here. Too much task conflict and a team will never agree on anything and will not get anything done. Too little task conflict and teams risk entering into groupthink, which can be dangerous.

The Dangers of Groupthink

Groupthink is when a team values perceived harmony above all else. They believe that getting along by agreeing is more important than reaching their goals, getting to the best decision, or innovating. The problem is the sense of harmony is an illusion. It looks like harmony because no one disagrees with the others, but internally not everyone agrees. They have different opinions; they just do not speak up because they do not want to "rock the boat."

Unfortunately, bad things happen when teams never disagree or have a true discussion about a decision. There have been numerous instances where top teams have entered a state of groupthink and ended up making such bad decisions that people died. For instance, the NASA Space Shuttle *Challenger* explosion is, in part, blamed on groupthink.

On January 28, 1986, I was in fifth grade. That Tuesday, before lunch, our teacher ushered us out to the playground to watch the space shuttle launch. Growing up in Orlando, Florida, just forty-eight miles from the Kennedy Space Center, we often went outside to watch the space shuttles launch. It was a gorgeous blue-sky day, but colder than usual. As with most Floridians, my thickest jacket was a sweatshirt. My classmates and I bounced around trying to stay warm in the cold air.

As we looked east, we soon saw the bright whitish-yellow trail of flames above the trees. We craned our necks as the shuttle went higher. Then there was an explosion and two white trails of smoke, like the top of a Y, split off. I did not understand what happened, but I knew that was not what shuttle launches typically looked like.

As we filed back into our classroom, our teacher Mrs. Whitney wheeled out the TV cart and turned on the news. We soon learned the space shuttle had exploded. There were no survivors.

This particular shuttle launch was special because Christa McAuliffe, a teacher from New Hampshire, was aboard as part of the Teacher in Space Project. NASA wanted to spark more interest in space exploration among American students and teachers. She was to be the first civilian in space.

After the accident, US President Ronald Reagan ordered the formation of a special committee, and there was extensive research into what caused the *Challenger* explosion. The technical malfunction had to do with a failed O-ring seal in the solid rocket booster. When fuel leaked past the O-ring, it caused the explosion.[6] However, the full story is much deeper.

NASA's organizational culture and decision-making progress were ultimately blamed.[7] Engineers had raised concerns about the O-ring being operational at lower temperatures. Up until the *Challenger* launch, the coldest weather during a shuttle launch was fifty-three degrees Fahrenheit. As the sun rose on January 28 there were icicles hanging off the space shuttle and by launch time it was only thirty-six degrees Fahrenheit, just four degrees above freezing.

In a phone call the evening before, a group from NASA and representatives from Morton Thiokol, the company that built the O-ring, discussed the possibility of the O-ring failing in cold temperatures, causing fuel to leak out and explode. Although the data leaned toward it failing, it was not definitive because it had not been tested. Morton Thiokol representatives expressed their concerns. Thiokol engineer Allan McDonald wanted to postpone the flight. Instead of clearly stating something like, "We should not launch if it is below fifty-three degrees," he said, "Lower temperatures are in the direction of badness for both O-rings..." No one gave the "no-go" command. Instead, feeling pressure from the group, McDonald went along with the majority, a decision he later regretted.

The culture of NASA was highly data-driven. It required that if you wanted to stop a launch or comment on nearly anything, you needed data to back up your point. A sign on a wall at NASA quoted engineer and management consultant W. Edwards Deming: "In God we trust. All others must bring data." There were concerns that the O-ring would fail at a low temperature, but there was no explicit data to verify the problem. You cannot have data for every single thing. Sometimes you have to extrapolate and use your imagination. The problem was not data. The problem was groupthink.

Several factors affect groupthink.[8] Two played a particularly significant role with the *Challenger* explosion. One of them is that groupthink is most common when there is pressure to agree. Because of many delays, NASA was under tremendous pressure to move forward with the launch, including pressure directly from the US president. NASA was supposed to launch a space shuttle at least once per month and up to fifty times per year. Several customers were sending payloads up on the shuttle and were pushing the launches to move forward. For instance, the US Department of Defense wanted to send up defense satellites, others were sending planetary probes that had narrow launch windows, and external customers paid for communication satellites to be up in space. This pressure made it harder to stall a launch because the O-ring might not work.

Groupthink is also more common in situations where a history of success leads to an inflated sense that nothing will go wrong. Before the *Challenger* launch, NASA had thirty-eight successful space flights and no loss of life since 1967, when three astronauts died in the *Apollo 1* test flight.

I discussed the *Challenger* accident with NASA engineer Michael Ciannilli, who started the *Apollo, Challenger, Columbia* Lessons Learned Program in 2016.[9] There were nineteen

Welcome task conflict because disagreements can lead to deeper thinking around creative challenges.

years between the *Apollo 1* and *Challenger* disasters. Then, seventeen years lapsed between the *Challenger* and *Columbia* accidents. This is just about a generation. In that time, many people retired and new employees joined. Knowledge and experience were lost. This lapse of time and loss of knowledge and experience made it easy to make mistakes again.

I asked Ciannilli what changed in the years since the *Challenger* explosion and whether the culture of groupthink had evolved. He said that when he was a NASA test director, which is like the conductor for the launch countdown, he encouraged gut checks, which are the opposite of data. Even if all the launch requirements were checked off, he asked the team, "Does it feel right?"

Ciannilli did delay a launch countdown once because of a gut check. A problem required resetting and rebooting the computers, which was a time-consuming process. There was a potential workaround, but as he talked with the engineers about whether it was a viable option, he heard a lot of "maybes." The launch involved loading cryogenic propellants on board, and a mistake would be particularly dangerous. During the back-and-forth about whether the newly proposed workaround procedure should be enacted, Ciannilli evoked *Challenger*'s name to push his perspective that they should delay. They did delay. They launched on a later date without issue. Ciannilli said he will never know if that procedure might have worked safely, but it was not worth the unnecessary risk. They certainly did not have a groupthink problem. They disagreed and decided through debate. That is what is important.

Groupthink means that getting along and agreeing on everything are more important than successfully reaching goals, more important than being creative, and more important than getting to the best decision. This is what happens when there is not enough conflict, in an environment that does not encourage some level of conflict. Poor decisions might be made even when some members of the team do not agree with them. A Deliberate Creative Team needs to be healthy enough to engage in some conflict and avoid groupthink. If it means delaying a launch, it might also mean saving a life.

On the other end of the spectrum, if a team is constantly in conflict and they disagree about everything all the time, they are not going to make decisions and nothing will get done. Playing devil's advocate has limited use and should be avoided in most cases or used sparingly. For innovation and creativity, you want a moderate level of task conflict. For instance, when a bunch of ideas are on the table, you can debate and disagree, and you can discuss which of these ideas might be the best for your team to move forward with. When a team listens to different perspectives, they will end up making a better decision. This sweet spot that a team is aiming for is called creative abrasion.

Creative Abrasion

In 1983, the Japanese car company Nissan opened its first US-based factory in Smyrna, Tennessee. Jerry Hirshberg, a designer with General Motors (GM), was hired to lead the new Nissan Design International facility. After sixteen years at GM and as the chief designer of Buick, Hirshberg was eager to be in a new environment without the prison of corporate bureaucratic limitations. He was charged with merging Japanese technical agility with American intuition and innovation. He approached the job with vigor and planned to design the entire organization with a focus on the creative process.

Soon Hirshberg was immersed in contrasting cultures. There were different perspectives on work hours, appropriate work attire, what quality work meant, and even what radio station to listen to. Hirshberg loved it. In his book *The Creative*

Priority, he wrote, "All of this I saw as a rich and yeasty opportunity for a kind of friction I wanted to turn into light rather than heat."[10] He knew he needed to create space for differing perspectives and experiences to merge without letting one culture dominate.

Throughout his time at Nissan, Hirshberg recognized the value of conflict to drive collaboration. He eventually coined "creative abrasion" as the term to describe just the right amount of task conflict in creative teams. Creative abrasion is the ability of teams to bring together conflicting views, friction, and polarities in a positive way to further enhance creative outcomes. He stated, "Rather than trying to reduce the friction that naturally arises between people working together by diluting or compromising positions, creative abrasion calls for the development of leadership styles that focus on first identifying and then incorporating polarized viewpoints... Recognizing, marking, and transforming pregnant moments of friction and collision into opportunities for breakthroughs are the work of creative abrasion."[11]

Later, Dr. Linda Hill from the Harvard Business School led a study examining creative abrasion and further pointed out, "It can and often does involve heartfelt disagreement, but not always. Abrasion in essence means simply that ideas and options compete for the best idea to emerge."[12] Conflict does not have to be a heated debate or involve passionate arguing. Anger and frustration do not need to be involved. It could simply be someone saying "I see that differently" and then sharing their perspective. Or intentionally asking others for their perspectives, such as "Lucia, what do you think of this idea?"

Several years ago, I was hired by a large university to assist with a huge change project. They were changing their entire human resources (HR) system, including pay structure, titles, how promotions occurred, hiring practices, everything. There were a dozen teams and each team was to examine an area of HR and recommend changes. I led two of the teams.

In one of the teams, the group was respectful and cordial with each other. They listened and responded, but after a few weeks, I realized we were not getting anywhere because everyone was being too nice. No one would disagree with anyone. There was no task conflict. I sensed no one wanted to upset or offend anyone else. I knew if we continued like this our results would be mediocre at best.

I assigned them an article to read about the value of conflict in teams and how it promotes more innovation. At the next meeting, we discussed the article and the team's energy shifted. They fully embraced the concept and started disagreeing more openly. They stopped holding back. They still showed respect by listening to one another and asking naive and probing questions—and they also challenged one another and offered different perspectives. It was beautiful.

We progressed a ton, and later executives praised this team as exemplary, with excellent results. We would not have achieved those results without developing a shared understanding of the value of task conflict.

By contrast, on the other team I worked with, one person continually argued about everything. She was also vice president of the union and approached the group and potential changes as threatening. For example, she demanded we never use the word "trust" when talking about the team. Her toxic approach pulled our team down, and we struggled to produce anything meaningful.

You want your team to engage in creative abrasion. There are many ways to facilitate the sharing of differing opinions. The activity later in this chapter provides a simple method to invite all team members to share.

How You Meet Matters

Open communication between team members increases psychological safety and trust, as well as creative abrasion. Sharing knowledge, information, and ideas is critical for teams to develop new solutions to challenges and innovate when needed.

For many teams, a big part of open communication takes place during team meetings. Team meetings are the time when the full team is together, usually focused on their work and the present challenges. Whether it is a special meeting convened to explore a problem or a regular weekly meeting, the norms, structures, and expectations of those meetings will play a big role in a team's ability to innovate together. Let's compare two examples of team meetings. In both examples imagine a team of ten people, in person, gathered around a large rectangular table.

In the first example, the teammates gather, politely saying hi to each other. They chat a little bit, but overall the room is fairly quiet. They begin on time with the team leader passing out agendas and welcoming them. During the meeting, each team member shares an update on their work and how their sub-team is doing. After each person shares, an occasional clarifying question follows but no additional conversation. As the hour nears its end, the leader thanks the team for its great work and ends the meeting. Everyone gathers their laptops and there is a bit of small talk, but team members file back to their respective desks in relative quiet.

In the second example, the team gathers with lots of smiles and a few fist bumps. One pair walks in while deep in a conversation that started in the hallway. Others are asking their colleagues questions about their weekend or talking about a project they are working on. The leader shared the agenda the day before and asked team members to show up prepared to discuss a particular issue. As the meeting begins, some team members pull out the agenda they printed. Their copies have notes scribbled in the margins.

The leader starts by asking the team a question, and each person answers it out loud while others listen. The question is related to work but provides an opportunity for people to share their perspectives and learn a little more about one another. For this component of the meeting, sometimes the leader brings in props, such as Climer Cards or other engagement tools. The leader then projects the team's task tracker on a screen and notes that nearly everyone is on track with their tasks that are leading to the quarterly goals. A brief conversation with two people who are slightly behind digs into what type of support they need. They share the roadblocks they ran into, and one of them asks for help. Another team member volunteers, and they agree to talk after the meeting.

After these preliminary but important components, the leader guides the team to the main topic. During the conversation, every team member comments, not in a round-robin style but rather members speak up and share when they are ready. Team members ask questions of the clarifying and the probing types, to better understand whoever is presenting and to push their thinking.

Occasional moments of silence naturally occur and give space for additional thought. At the same time, the group has robust energy and is engaged. Before the meeting ends, they discuss the next steps. One team member records the next steps in a shared digital tool, while someone else adds a few new tasks to the task tracker. As the meeting ends, team members feel satisfied and motivated. They did not solve the issue, but they better understand it and that is progress. Everyone knows what they need to do to prepare for their next meeting,

Meetings are an important time of collaboration and **an opportunity to be creative together.**

where they will take another step toward resolving the issue. The team members depart and an energy fills the air as they return to their desks or head to other meetings.

ONE BIG DIFFERENCE between these groups is in how their meeting structure affects the team dynamics, and therefore their ability to be creative together. If you use your team meeting as the time for each person to update the rest of the team on their progress, you may be missing an opportunity for a group of smart people to meld their creative minds and solve real problems. Deliberate Creative Teams view meetings as an important time of collaboration and an opportunity to be creative together. They understand the importance of preparing for the meeting in advance so they can bring new ideas, questions, and curiosities that will push the team forward.

How Much Did That Meeting Cost?

Meetings are an important time for teams. They present an opportunity to build psychological safety, engage in creative abrasion, and communicate diverse perspectives. Very few leaders think about how meetings are designed, yet the structures and processes used in meetings are critical for developing a Deliberate Creative Team. We will talk more about the processes in the next chapter, but let's first look at how much a team meeting costs.

If a team has ten people and the average salary is $100,000 per year, then each person is making roughly $50 per hour. A one-hour meeting costs the company $500 (ten people times $50 each). Is a progress update worth $500? It might be, but if you could do that for a fraction of the cost with the same outcome, wouldn't that be worth it?

In addition, professionals spend a lot of time in meetings. On average, each week CEOs spend eighteen hours in meetings, civil servants twenty-two hours, office workers sixteen hours, and engineers about fifteen hours.[13] That means between one-third and one-half of an employee's salary is for meetings. You want to make sure that time is well spent so you can use the power of human collaboration to generate new ideas, work through the best solutions, and solve problems to serve your clients. Meetings can be a powerful tool for creative collaboration if they are well designed. They can also suck the life out of you! Plan meetings so that you are using the time well.

Meeting Space, Meeting Time

In 2012, Sandy Pentland from MIT reported an interesting study in the *Harvard Business Review*. Pentland and his team designed special badges that collect sociometric data from the wearer. The badges track one hundred points of data per minute, including "what tone of voice they use; whether they face one another; how much they gesture; how much they talk, listen, and interrupt; and even their levels of extroversion and empathy."[14]

Over several years the team gathered data and measured communication patterns of about 2,500 people in twenty-one organizations, for up to six weeks at a time. This produced a huge amount of data about how teams interact.

There were two particularly interesting results related to communication. One was that the most effective teams face each other. Literally. When someone is talking, others in the group physically turn to them to listen. It seems so simple, almost elementary, but it makes sense. It conveys to both the speaker and the listener a sense of engagement. You can facilitate this with a team by setting up the chairs to be in a circle (or something like it). Closing laptop screens helps too.

The badges also revealed that high-performing teams share talking time almost equally. Throughout a meeting, for instance, no one person dominates the conversation. If a team of ten people is meeting for sixty minutes, that means each person talks for approximately six minutes during the meeting. This rule has exceptions, but one can easily imagine a scenario in which a team engaged like this solves problems.

Years ago when I was working for a university, the dean came to one of our staff meetings. He began by saying he was joining us to get our ideas about a new initiative. He proceeded to share some details. I was rapt with attention and eager to contribute. I picked up my pen and jotted down a couple of thoughts while I waited for him to pause. Fifteen minutes passed and he was still going. I started to look around the table. I caught the eye of one colleague and we seemed to read each other's minds, wondering when he was going to stop. I nearly burst out laughing and had to look down at my paper. I started doodling. He continued his monologue for fifty-five minutes, stood up, thanked us for our thoughts, and left. Seriously. I cannot make this up!

That meeting stood out to me so much because typically our team meetings were balanced. Of the ten people on the team, every person spoke at every meeting (and we did not do report-outs). There was a true sense of contribution and the sharing of ideas. We would bounce perspectives around, change our minds, and emerge with something better. We were creative and provided quality services to our students. It was a joy to work with that team.

Activity: Balance Participation

Purpose: invite different perspectives and balance participation

Time: five minutes or more

Materials: none

In a team meeting, you may find that some people talk more than others. This may be somewhat natural, depending on each person's introverted or extroverted tendencies. However, you want to build a culture where everyone participates. They are on the team to contribute, after all.

One way to set the tone that everyone is expected to speak and engage is to kick off meetings by asking each person to share something. Make it relevant to the work, not something frivolous or pointless. (Adults do not like that.) For instance, if the team meeting is about the budget, ask each person to share a hope they have for the next year's budget. Think about a question that will drive valuable conversation later in the meeting. Note that if you wait until thirty minutes in to do this, it is too late. By then, you will have already taught them that this is a place to sit back and listen. By including each person's voice at the beginning, the later conversation may also be more balanced. Having started with it, you can come back to this method any time you want everyone's input, not just at the beginning.

Avoid Being Insular

While internal team communication is important, like many things in life it is best in moderation. If team members communicate too much with each other and only with each other, they become too insular. They need exposure to diverse perspectives. Team members need to communicate with those outside their team.

In 2009, Ute R. Hülsheger from Maastricht University in the Netherlands led a meta-analysis study analyzing which team variables impact innovation in the workplace. The researchers found that "if individuals maintain social relations with people outside their core work team, they are more likely to be exposed to new kinds of information and diverse viewpoints and thus generate fresh ideas."[15] You want team members to chat in the hallway, ask each other questions during their workweek, and bounce ideas around as needed. You also need them to interact with people outside the team— and even outside the company—to get new ideas.

In addition, communication that is too centralized can also decrease creative performance.[16] For instance, if team members must always relay information through a supervisor or other person, or if approval needs to be given for nearly everything, they will stop asking and therefore stop innovating. The process is too cumbersome. Impromptu direct communication is essential for creativity. Communication that must always be directed through specific channels or can occur only in formal meetings inhibits the sharing of spontaneous ideas, asking quick questions, and fostering ideation.

Working virtually can make this particularly challenging, and that is why communication tools like Slack and messaging platforms have been so effective. They allow us to easily talk with each other and share insights and resources without being too intrusive.

Communication is tough. Most people think they are good communicators. In over fifteen years of consulting, I have only met a few people who admitted to being poor communicators. Assessing whether you are an effective communicator is a challenge. One of the best ways is through feedback, but understanding and incorporating the feedback into your work and life takes skill and a dose of humility. You can get that feedback in a multitude of ways: anonymous surveys, 360-degree evaluations, asking colleagues through one-on-one interviews, and audio- or video-recording yourself in meetings (with permission of those present, of course).

As a consultant, I was once asked to help an executive team of a health care company improve their communication. They wanted me to video their team meetings and then provide feedback on how they could improve. I provided some insightful perspectives, but the biggest problem was that the team was so nervous about being on camera and being evaluated that they were not being themselves. They sat up extra straight, did not fidget and barely moved, and they were measured and professional in their responses. I am not sure it resulted in the sincere feedback they wanted. Had they been able to truly relax and be themselves, it would have been gold.

TEAM DYNAMICS are the most complex element of building a creative team. Improving them can be a lot of work and requires looking at your team with a fresh perspective and trying some new things.

Team dynamics and the team creative process are tightly connected. Together the two elements drive collaboration. In the next chapter, you will learn some specific tools and techniques that will generate creative ideas and innovative solutions, while also fostering positive team dynamics.

6

The Transformative Power of Team Creative Process

ONE PERVASIVE MYTH is that creativity requires wild abandon or recklessness and that too many constraints inhibit creativity. In reality, creativity, and especially innovation, follows a fairly consistent, structured process that involves identifying a problem or challenge, finding solutions, and then implementing one or more of those solutions. Learning this process was a huge aha experience for me. I realized that most teams are doomed because they do not even know a creative process exists. I did not know there was a creative process until at least ten years into my career. What a loss! My teams missed out on so much potential because we never talked about how to be creative together. We never had training or even a short lesson on how to brainstorm new ideas. We never discussed steps to being creative or activities that could enhance our results. Sigh. With this book, you and your teams will not miss out the way I did. You are going to learn a process called creative problem solving and be able to guide your teams from problem to implementation.

The creative process includes a series of operations, actions, norms, tools, and techniques, as well as the spirit in which they are approached.[1] The process is the method of working together. This includes the way team meetings are structured, the way the agenda is designed (if there is one), how you track progress on tasks, your approach to projects, how new ideas get considered, and more.

The way a team approaches a problem affects its ability to be creative. Understanding and using a creative process may be the crux of your team's ability to innovate on demand. Team purpose and team dynamics are important, and when you establish the creative process, purpose and dynamics become easier. In this chapter I am going to teach you a creative process you can use anytime you want to innovate. Put this into practice and you will generate worthwhile solutions when needed.

Diverge, Then Converge

Understanding the difference between divergent and convergent thinking and when to use each is foundational to the creative process. Divergent thinking is about generating lots of ideas and perspectives. It is when you think big and bold. You go in different directions and follow various tangents. It may occur in a free-flowing or spontaneous manner. It is the classic brainstorming technique where wild, wacky ideas arise.

Convergent thinking is where you narrow all the ideas down to the best ones. You evaluate and critique; you compare and analyze. The focus is on looking for the one "right" answer. All of us use both divergent and convergent thinking, but the key is to be deliberate about which one you are using and when.[2]

When you are in a brainstorming session and someone blurts out "That will never work!" they are moving from a divergent state (generating the ideas) to a convergent state (evaluating the ideas). The convergent comment influences everyone else's thinking and soon everyone is in the convergent mindset; shifting back into a divergent mode becomes difficult. The problem many teams face is that they do not know the difference between the two types of thinking, and they try to engage in both at the same time. Physically, the brain can only do one type of thinking at a time.

The other challenge is that most of us have been trained since we were kids to be good at convergent thinking. Every standardized test, every multiple-choice question, every instance when one right answer is required encourages convergent thinking. For instance, in elementary school, you were probably given worksheets that included problems like $5 + 5 = \_\_$. There is only one right answer. It is a convergent thinking question. But what if the worksheet said $\_\_ + \_\_ = 10$? Now there are several options and it requires a more divergent approach.

Growing up, how many times did you have a divergent thinking test question that was something like, "List all the reasons for ____"? Or "Provide all the possible ways for ____"? Whenever I lead a creativity training or keynote, I ask the audience to raise their hands if they remember a test question like this. Usually one or two people do, and their experience was so unusual that they can remember the teacher and the test topic. Sometimes they even remember the exact test question!

Fast-forwarding to adulthood, how many times at work is there only one right answer to a problem? Almost never. When has a senior leader given you a multiple-choice question about your work? Our mainstream education system (at least in the United States) is about teaching facts and the right answers. Our professional world is about solving problems with creative solutions. This disconnect leads to all sorts of issues in the workplace.

We are trained in one way and then asked to be another once we "grow up." If you feel like you are not creative or that you struggle with generating new ideas, you are not to blame. Creativity has been trained out of you. The same is true for your team members. You all need to be retrained in divergent thinking.

The good news is that you can train yourself and your team to be proficient in generating new perspectives. It is all about learning to think divergently. I have three tips for enhancing your team's divergent thinking skills.

Be clear about your mode. One of the best ways you can think more divergently is to be clear with yourself and your team about when you want to engage in divergent thinking and when you want to engage in convergent thinking. Designate a certain amount of time for diverging. When the time is up, move into converging and evaluating the ideas. Holding back on criticism in the moment is easier if team members know they will get to evaluate the ideas later. Generating ideas and evaluating the ideas are equally important parts of the process.

Use a variety of techniques. Mix it up beyond the classic brainstorming. Using a variety of ideation tools and techniques stimulates different parts of your brain and leads to more diverse ideas. There are dozens, even hundreds, of ideation tools you can use, for example brainwriting, SCAMPER, associations, and forced connections. (For more techniques, visit climerconsulting.com/extras.)

Follow the divergent thinking guidelines. These guidelines were created in 1948 by Alex Osborn, who also developed brainstorming (more on him in a minute). They promote staying in that divergent space and ideating more readily. The guidelines are:

- **Suspend judgment.** The key word here is "suspend." Do not evaluate the ideas at first, including your own. You will get to judge them in the convergent phase.

- **Seek wild ideas.** You never know what the next best idea will be. The wilder you get, the better.

- **Combine and build on ideas.** One of the great values of collaboration is you can combine and build on each other's ideas, perspectives, and brilliance.

- **Go for quantity.** Quantity leads to quality. You are ultimately looking for the best ideas, but chances are the best idea is not the first one or even the tenth. Aim for one hundred ideas. Maybe ten of them are excellent, and you will not have them if you stop too soon. Keep going and push yourself to generate more ideas.

When diverging, I find it inspiring to keep these guidelines on a wall poster or a cheat sheet at the table. The next time you want your team to generate new ideas, start by discussing divergent thinking and explain the divergent thinking guidelines. (You can download a free cheat sheet with the divergent thinking guidelines at climerconsulting.com/extras.)

Creative Problem Solving: The Process

We are going to get into the creative problem solving process, but before we do, a brief explanation. What you will learn is a four-stage process you can follow to be more creative. A process is a series of steps to achieve a certain end. Within

Divergent thinking is about generating lots of ideas and perspectives. **Convergent thinking is where you narrow down the best ideas.**

this process, there are tools and techniques to use at each step. Tools are devices designed to carry out a function. For instance, if you are paddling down a river, then your canoe and canoe paddle are both tools. Your success will depend on how you use them, which is the technique.

When it comes to technique, creativity is a lot like canoeing. I have been teaching canoeing for most of my adult life, and I am a whitewater canoe instructor for the North Carolina Outward Bound School. Most people I have taught to canoe were introduced to canoeing as a kid, maybe at summer camp or on a family vacation. They show up to their lesson confident and thinking they know what to do. On a calm, blue-sky, sunny day they have no problem paddling across a pond. Put them in a moving river and soon they are spinning in circles, getting stuck on shallow sections, tipping upside down, and then cursing their canoe partner as they swim through a rapid. They do not know a single proper stroke, they hold the paddle incorrectly, and they cannot read the water.

As I watch them paddle through the current and switch their paddle to the other side of the canoe, my face scrunches up, my shoulders tense, and I say to myself, "No, no, no, no, no." Then I am furiously paddling into the rapid to guide their empty boat and flailing bodies back to shore. They have the tools, but their technique is horrible. They do not know what they do not know. Often they have to unlearn misinformation they heard as a kid.

Creativity is the same. It is one of those things that look easy, but until we understand the process and the technique we flail around and tend to blame other team members for our lack of innovation.

To progress in this work, you need to move past blame and get serious about learning the creative process, new tools, and techniques.

ONE OF the big findings from the last century of creativity research is that humans naturally follow a creative process. Across our species, we seem to take a relatively similar approach to solving problems, and this applies to a wide range of situations. However, it can take a lot of intentional trial and error to figure out what that process is. You are going to short-cut that trial and error and stand on the shoulders of all the brilliant, creative giants who have come before you.

All creative processes involve identifying a problem or challenge, finding solutions, and then implementing one or more of those solutions. Creative problem solving (CPS) is a process designed to codify our natural creative process. The CPS process was first developed by Alex Osborn in the 1950s. Osborn was intrigued by creativity and was part of BBDO, one of the top marketing firms of the time (the O is for Osborn). In 1948, he published a book called *Your Creative Power* in which he introduced the concept of brainstorming. The book quickly became popular, it went "viral" as we say today, and brainstorming soon became a well-known concept. In 1953, Osborn published *Applied Imagination*, popularizing creative problem solving. The following year Osborn paired up with Dr. Sidney Parnes from Buffalo State University in New York to create a method for educating others about using CPS. Over the years CPS has been heavily researched and refined down to four main stages:

1   **Clarify.** Clarifying is about narrowing in on the specific goal, wish, or challenge that will be explored. This includes gathering data and determining the questions that will lead to solutions.

2   **Ideate.** Generating ideas to solve the challenge.

3   **Develop.** Selecting and further refining the few promising ideas that will lead to solutions.

4 **Implement.** Identifying resources needed, actions to be taken, and how to overcome hurdles related to implementing the best idea(s). Then, getting started.[3]

CREATIVE PROBLEM SOLVING

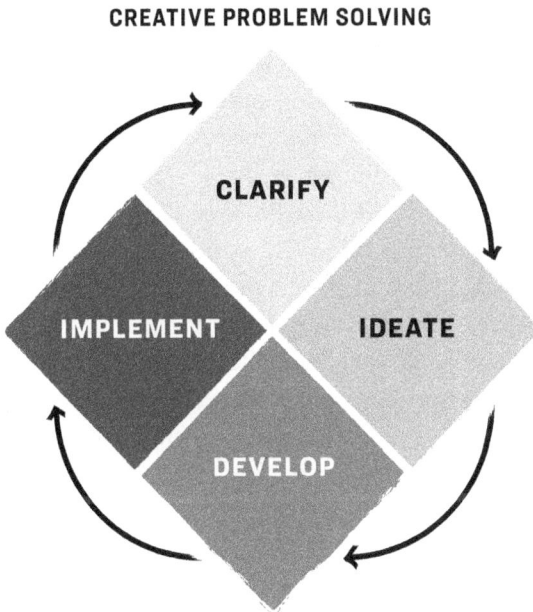

Teams who use CPS can be more creative and generate more innovative solutions. For smaller problems, the entire process might take an hour. For bigger problems, the process might take months or even years, with small cycles of the process happening throughout.

As individuals, we each have a propensity for one or more of the stages in creative problem solving. We tend to want to stay in that stage and may even skip the other stages altogether.[4] So you need to be mindful to engage with the entire model.

In each of the four stages, you will start off in divergent thinking mode and move into convergent thinking.

Let's dig into each of these stages and how you can use them with your team.

Creative Problem Solving: Clarify

One of the common challenges we face when solving problems is that we often have an inaccurate sense of the real problem. We think we know what it is, but we are often wrong. The good news is that spending as little as five minutes clarifying the problem to better understand the situation will significantly increase your chance of finding solutions that will make a positive difference.

In his book *Solve the Real Problem*, Dr. Roger Firestien, a professor at Buffalo State University's Center for Applied Creativity, describes four steps to clarifying: identify the challenge, gather data about the situation, redefine the problem, and choose a creative question that will generate new ideas.[5]

To identify the goal, wish, or challenge to address, you can do something as simple as repeatedly completing the phrase "I wish..." or "Wouldn't it be nice if..." with a different ending each time. Try swapping out verbs or nouns. For instance, use the verb "design" in one sentence and "create" in another. While they may be synonyms, they do not mean exactly the same thing. In reviewing the phrases you generate, you may spot one phrase that most accurately portrays the problem.

Having identified what you want to tackle, you then gather data to gain a greater understanding of the situation. This includes quantitative, qualitative, and anecdotal data. Depending on the topic, the data gathering could range from a quick search online to a few short conversations to extensive research.

Once you have a better understanding of the situation, you may notice you are looking at the problem differently. Be open to this shift. This is the value of the clarify stage. You may realize that what you thought was the problem was not quite right and you need to shift the big question you are asking.

From here you want to generate a list of open-ended, creative questions to redefine the problem (divergent thinking). Experiment with different iterations, but start the questions with one of these phrases: "How might we/I...," "In what ways might...," or "What are all the ways..." For more details, see the activity below.

Finally, decide which question best fits your challenge (convergent thinking). The way you phrase your question affects the type of ideas you get. Therefore, review your list and choose one or more questions that will lead to the ideas you are looking for.

Remember the scenario from chapter 4 about the learning and development team that needed to design a new onboarding program for new hires? If that team was enacting the clarify stage of this process, its list of challenge questions might include these:

- How might we design a new onboarding program so that new hires feel welcomed and connected to our company?

- What are all the ways we might welcome new hires in with open arms?

- How might our team lead a company-wide program that trains supervisors how to onboard their new staff?

- In what ways might we onboard new remote employees so they feel connected before their first day of work?

- How might we modify our existing onboarding program to increase a sense of inclusion?

We could continue with a long list. I usually recommend aiming for ten to twenty-five challenge questions and then picking one that is the best fit for the situation. By the end of the clarify stage, you will have one question that you take into the ideate stage.

Activity: "Might" Is a Mighty Word

Purpose: to use powerful words that invite creativity and generate the best question for the problem

Time: ten minutes

Materials: none

Often when we want ideas, we ask questions like, "What should we do?" or "How can we fix that?" The problem is that words like "should," "could," "can," "do," and "will" imply that you are looking for one right answer. You shift into a convergent thinking mode. Instead, you want to open up the possibilities. You want to be in a divergent mode.

Try rephrasing your question using the word "might." For instance, compare these two examples:

- How *should* we eliminate racism in our community?
- How *might* we eliminate racism in our community?

This is such a complex problem that to think there is one right solution is ridiculous. If we hear the word "should," there is an implicit understanding that there is one right answer and the brain starts to search for that answer and closes off possibilities. When we hear the word "might," our brains interpret that as an invitation for exploration.

Try to shift your language in everyday use. Pay attention to how you ask questions. For the next two days see if you can ask at least five questions using the word "might." Instead of "How should we design our retreat to get the outcomes we want?" try "How might we design our retreat to get the outcomes we want?" It might feel awkward at first. It will probably feel more cumbersome to you than it sounds to the listener. Sometimes when you are growing and experimenting, you have to embrace the awkwardness.

When you are responding to an idea, you can also use questions to replace the word "no." Instead of "No, that's not in our budget," ask "How might we do this given our limited budget?"

It also works remarkably well with teenagers: Instead of "No, you can't do that. That is way too dangerous," ask "How might you do that in a way that is safe?"

The difference is subtle but significant. As you try this with colleagues, friends, or family members, notice how it shifts the tenor of the conversation. Does it decrease defensiveness? Did you feel more openness in the conversation? Did it lead to new ideas?

Creative Problem Solving: Ideate

Once you have clarified the problem, it is time to move to the ideate stage. Your ultimate goal is to identify the best idea(s) to solve the challenge. To do that, let go of the focus on "best" for a moment. Start in the divergent mode and focus on *lots* of ideas. Because, as you now know, quantity leads to quality. When we generate ideas, our first ideas are the most typical. We need to push past those first few to get to the good stuff. Most groups stop with less than ten ideas. One client told me her team always went with the first idea that someone shared, no matter what it was. As you can imagine, that could be problematic.

If your first ten ideas are typical, your next ten will be a little better, and your third ten ideas will be more unique. This concept is called the third third. Even though thirty ideas are better than ten, if you can push even further to seventy-five or one hundred ideas, the third third concept still applies. Your third third of ideas will be more creative than your first third. You may be surprised by how quickly you can generate lots of ideas. Getting to one hundred ideas is much easier than you might think. However, I recommend you avoid brainstorming altogether.

A Brief History of Brainstorming

There are dozens, probably hundreds, of ideation techniques. Brainstorming is one of them. Most people use the term "brainstorming" to mean coming up with new ideas, but brainstorming is a specific technique with set guidelines developed by Osborn. In his book *Your Creative Power*, he describes the process where a small group gets together with the intent to generate ideas for a common challenge. The group shouts out ideas and the facilitator writes them down. It is a free flow, but with some guidelines.

He instructed readers to use the divergent thinking rules mentioned earlier and insisted that having a facilitator was critical. Osborn claimed that "properly organized and run, a group can be a goldmine of ideas." [6] After *Your Creative Power* popularized the technique in the 1950s, researchers began studying the impact of brainstorming. Does it really work? Sometimes.

I do not remember when I first learned to brainstorm. Do you? It seems nearly everyone is expected to know how to brainstorm even though most people have never been taught. Therefore, most of us have had mixed experiences brainstorming with groups—some good but mostly bad. During keynote speeches when I talk about bad brainstorming sessions, I see a lot of vigorously nodding heads, furrowed brows, and angst-filled faces. Nearly everyone has experienced a lousy brainstorming session that felt like a waste of time. If you have been in some fun, productive, energetic brainstorms where lots of ideas were generated, you are in the minority. I have never once seen a group of people without training specifically about how to brainstorm well have a successful brainstorming session.

The way you phrase a question **affects the type of ideas you get.**

Here is the good news. Learning to brainstorm well is not a top priority for increasing your team's creativity. In fact, studies from 1958, 1978, and 1996 all reported limitations on the effectiveness of brainstorming.[7] A study in 1958, sponsored by the Office of Naval Research and conducted by Yale University, compared ideas brainstormed by twelve groups composed of four students each to the ideas generated by forty-eight individual students working alone, whose ideas were organized into twelve random groups.[8]

The important takeaway from this research, for our purposes, is that it showed that the ideas from individuals working alone were better and more diverse than ideas generated through groups using brainstorming. But that does not fit with what we know about teams and innovation.

Twenty years later Tudor Rickards and B.L. Freedman analyzed multiple brainstorming studies and found the same results. They also criticized the brainstorming studies up to that point because they all involved experimental conditions and none reported on real, practical groups.[9] The groups being studied were not actually teams. They were just groups of people thrown together for a brief experiment. Big difference.

Finally, in 1996 Robert I. Sutton and Andrew Hargadon from Stanford University answered the call to study real groups and analyzed IDEO, one of the leading design firms in the United States and a big user of Osborn's brainstorming methods.[10] Sutton and Hargadon conducted a qualitative study to gain a deeper understanding of how IDEO used brainstorming within their organization.

A facilitator leads IDEO's brainstorming sessions. This is an important distinction. Researchers found that when a brainstorming group had a facilitator, the number of unique ideas jumped by 700 percent (from twenty-three ideas to an average of 167)![11] I regularly see groups generate between one hundred and two hundred ideas when I facilitate a session with them. Like any tool, brainstorming is only as powerful as the technique used to implement it.

In summary, brainstorming works well under certain conditions. These include when:

- Group members know each other reasonably well and have a positive working relationship.

- The group has a reasonable level of expertise related to the topic.

- Group members are skilled at divergent thinking and generating ideas.

- Group members are motivated to generate new ideas for the challenge.

- A facilitator is leading the process.

In essence, successful group brainstorming involves skills and abilities in brainstorming techniques and social dynamics, as well as expertise in the topic. Brainstorming can be effective, but it all depends on context. If your group meets all the criteria above, then the classic brainstorming technique may be an effective ideation tool. If not, skip it and try some other techniques. (I have included several ideation techniques for you in the freebies at climerconsulting.com/extras.)

The good news is that you can become better at brainstorming, but I recommend avoiding the classic tool for now until your team has built up their divergent thinking skills.

Activity: Write It, Say It, Stick It

Purpose: to generate lots of ideas in a short time

Time: fifteen minutes

Materials: pens and sticky notes, or group access to a shared digital document (for example, a Google Doc or Mural)

When I start an ideation session, I almost always begin with this activity, which is best for a group that understands the divergent thinking guidelines and has finished the clarify stage: You have a clear challenge question, one that starts with a phrase like "How might we . . .?"

To start, I often provide a few tips on how to write a useful idea. For instance, start with a verb and add as much detail as you have. "Social media" is not a useful idea. It is just a noun. A more useful idea would be "Collaborate with our partners and design a social media campaign that focuses on stories from our audience."

Invite each person to write down as many ideas to respond to the question as they can in five minutes. If you are using pen and paper, write each idea on a separate sticky note. Write as fast as you can without judging your ideas. You are going for quantity, not quality. After five minutes, each person should have a small pile of sticky notes with ideas on them. If you are doing this online, everyone can add ideas to a shared document or use a collaboration tool like Mural.

Then invite each person to share their ideas out loud. If you are using sticky notes, post them on a wall so everyone can see them. If the team is writing ideas in a shared document, you might instead invite anyone to ask about an idea that is not clear. Keep this portion fast-paced and high-energy. In either format, while the group is sharing, encourage people to keep adding ideas. Avoid getting into conversations about each idea; just get them up on the wall or in the document. Repeat the process, if desired, or move to another ideation technique when finished. In a typical ideation session I try to use two to four techniques to bring in more diverse ideas and new thinking.

Ideas Are a Dime a Dozen

Ideas are everywhere and on their own they are virtually useless. You could put a hundred entrepreneurs in a room and give them the same idea and an hour to generate a business model based on that idea. You would likely get one hundred different answers. For instance, all restaurants essentially have the same idea. They cook food and serve it to people in exchange for money, but that idea is implemented in a million different ways. Think of all the restaurants you have been to in your life—the chain restaurant off the side of the highway, the fast-food joint, the cute café in your neighborhood, the nice place downtown where you need a reservation months in advance. They are each different, even if in subtle ways. They serve different types of food, have a different vibe, or do something special that makes them unique.

Ideas are important, but sometimes we have this misconception that the ideas alone are valuable. What is valuable is the vision and implementation related to an idea. Because we can overinflate our ideas, we sometimes keep them to ourselves out of fear that someone will "steal" them. This is rare. Bouncing ideas around with others makes them stronger than when we keep them caged away. Dani Chesson said it well in episode 91 of my podcast *The Deliberate Creative*: "All good ideas come from engaging and sharing your ideas with others."[12]

Years ago, I was at a networking event with business leaders and entrepreneurs. I started up a conversation with a guy I did not know and asked him about his work. He said he was starting a new business but could not talk about it because he

Do not treat your ideas like precious pieces of porcelain. Kick them around, bounce them off the walls. **They will only grow stronger.**

had to keep the new product private. I felt skeptical. I asked, "Oh wow! What is so private about this new product?"

"It's going to be a huge disruptor. I can't say what it is because I don't want you to steal my idea."

My eyes grew wider and I chuckled. "Me? You're worried about me stealing your idea?"

He backpedaled just a bit. "Well, you might tell someone else about it and then they might take it."

"Huh. I don't think anyone's going to steal your idea based on a short conversation at a networking event." I thought, "Why is this guy here? How is anyone supposed to get to know him, much less support him, if he won't share?" At this point, I was curious how the conversation might continue if I pushed a bit more. Because of his caginess, I thought for sure his idea must be about cybersecurity or nuclear weapons.

I asked, "What genre is your idea in?"

He said, "I guess I can tell you that. It's about smoothies."

"Smoothies? Like the drink?"

"Yes! This is going to revolutionize the smoothie industry!"

It took all my self-control to not burst out laughing. If he knew anything about me, he would know I would never be interested in pursuing any business idea related to the food industry. Although I enjoy a good smoothie, I do not like cooking. While smoothies are not exactly cooking, they do involve a kitchen, so I am out.

He then added, "We'll launch in about a year. You'll definitely notice us! It's going to be amazing!"

It has been at least ten years. I am still waiting.

The problem with keeping an idea to ourselves is that we have such a narrow, limited view that we cannot possibly fully develop it alone. Thinking that we have all the answers or that we can develop a big idea into a full solution without input is preposterous and egotistical. Do not treat your ideas like precious pieces of porcelain. Share your ideas with others. Kick them around, bounce them off the walls. They will not break. They will only get stronger over time as you mold them, gather input, and let them grow.

In 2011, I was developing Climer Cards. On one side of the deck are fifty-two watercolor paintings I did of simple images that can spark metaphors and ideas. I wanted the flip side of the cards to be used for a different activity, but I was not sure what. At the time, I was managing a team-building program in Madison, Wisconsin, that included a challenge course. I was part of a small group of managers of other challenge course programs called the Wisconsin Challenge Course Consortium. We met quarterly to share ideas and collectively make all our programs better. I brought the problem to the group and asked them to explore ideas with me. In less than thirty minutes, the flip side was designed. Today, each card has a number, shape, and color on it, which are used to sort the people using the cards into groups. For instance, you could sort a large group by shapes. All the circles would gather together, all the squares together, the triangles, et cetera. Then you could do the same thing with numbers or colors.

Facilitators love this extra perk. This same group also came up with the name Climer Cards (which I was resistant to at first). If I had kept my ideas to myself, I might not have landed on this excellent concept for the flip side of the deck. It was a simple idea that added immense value to the product.

Activity: Forced Connections

Purpose: to generate more ideas using a different technique

Time: fifteen to thirty minutes

Materials: one or more decks of Climer Cards Original and/ or Climer Cards 2, blank paper or sticky notes

Forced connections is a technique that pushes us to connect two unlikely things and use that connection to generate ideas. In this case, you are connecting your challenge with something unrelated. A great source for these unrelated objects is a deck of Climer Cards (either the Original Deck or Deck 2). Follow these simple steps:

1 Randomly pick a card.

2 Lay it on the table so everyone can see it.

3 Invite the group to think about how that object connects with the challenge.

4 Ask, "What ideas do you get from this image?"

5 As people share, be sure to capture the ideas in writing using sticky notes or whatever technique you have already been using.

6 After the group has generated a few ideas, flip to another image. I like to keep it moving at a fairly fast pace so the group doesn't get bored.

For instance, a group's challenge might be "What else might we offer in our yoga studio to bring in more clients?" You show them the Climer Card with the iron on it. Then someone says, "We could turn up the heat in the classroom and make it really hot. That would be particularly appealing during the middle of our cold Montana winters."

And hot yoga is born.

Just kidding. That is not how it really evolved, but it could have happened that way.

The concept here is to force a connection between two unlikely things. It is a great way to bring in new sources of inspiration from unexpected places.

Converging on the Best Ideas

After you generate lots of ideas, you need to shift into convergent thinking and select the best ones. You can do this in numerous ways, but voting works remarkably well. I like to give each person three to five little stickers and invite them to put a sticker by what they think are the best ideas to address the challenge. This is a good way to see which ideas rise to the top. Then look at those top ideas and select several to move into the develop stage. You want to take several ideas into the develop stage because you cannot know yet which ones will be the best solutions.

With voting, you are not using a strictly democratic process where this idea has five votes and that has four, so you are going with the one with five votes. The purpose is to see which ideas rise to the top. Instead, you can find a natural cutoff. You might consider any idea with a vote. Or if there are several with five, six, or seven votes, and one idea that has only one vote, then you might move forward only the ideas with at least five votes. You can also use voting to identify the best ideas and then have a conversation about the top ones.

Creative Problem Solving: Develop

When an idea first emerges, it is only as deep as what will fit on a sticky note. The idea is almost worthless because it is just a sentence or two. The develop stage is when you turn that idea into a true solution so it can be implemented. This is also when you start exploring whether the idea is worth pursuing. Exploring that in the develop stage is better than immediately moving to implementation.

Keep in mind that being creative means you are doing something novel. We tend to criticize what we are not familiar with or sure about. The develop stage works best when you avoid criticism and keep an open mind. The idea already passed the convergent thinking in the ideation stage. Now you need to develop it a little further to see if it is viable. A simple tool called PPCO (pluses, potentials, concerns, overcoming concerns) will guide you.[13]

Activity: PPCO

Purpose: to examine an idea in more depth and determine if it might be a potential solution

Time: fifteen to thirty minutes

Materials: the PPCO template (download at climerconsulting .com/extras)

Every idea has strengths and weaknesses. This process brings both to the surface so you better understand what the idea could be. It also prevents you from focusing only on the negatives, which people tend to do.

Write your idea at the top of the template or on a blank piece of paper. Answer these questions based on your idea:

- **Pluses:** What do you like about the idea? List at least three pluses or strengths of the idea.

- **Potentials:** What are the potentials of the idea? If you implemented this idea, what might happen? What might result from this idea?

- **Concerns:** No idea is perfect. What concerns or limitations does the idea have? Write them as a creative question starting with "How to ...?" or "How might ...?"

- **Overcoming concerns:** Generate some ideas to answer each concern. Focus on one concern at a time.

When I lead this activity with clients, someone often comments that by looking at the positives of the idea in addition to the concerns, they shift their thinking. They were going to dismiss an idea, but after doing PPCO they have a better understanding of the idea and how it might work.

Creative Problem Solving: Implement

At this point, you have identified and refined a challenge, generated new ideas, narrowed down to the best ideas, and developed them into solutions. Now, you must put those solutions into action. You must implement!

Moving a solution to implementation can be tricky. You need to figure out where to start, and you might need to get approval or convince others that the idea is worth implementing. One of the first things I consider is the smallest, simplest way I can begin. Can I prototype this idea on a small scale? Can I test it first with some friends? Can I sell it before it is fully complete?

When I was making the original deck of Climer Cards, I had no idea if facilitators would be interested enough to pay money for a deck of cards. Sure, I had about a dozen friends who told me it was a great idea, but they were biased. I was trying to figure out how to test the idea without spending the money to manufacture hundreds of decks. Fortunately, a friend told me about Kickstarter, a crowdfunding platform for launching creative projects. This was 2012, and Kickstarter was less than three years old. The way it works is that once you set up your campaign, you have a set amount of time to presell your product. If the campaign is successful, you get the funds to manufacture the product. The backers (those who contribute funds) get their product, usually after a long wait because it has to be manufactured. If the campaign is not successful, the backers get their money back and you get nothing. I had five weeks to presell $2,500 worth of Climer Cards. I still remember clicking the submit button to launch the project. I was so nervous. I had no idea if it would work.

Kickstarter was a game-changer for me. Within two days I got a phone call from the University of Wisconsin. They wanted to preorder eight decks for $200, but that was not listed as an option on my campaign. I had been thinking so small that it never occurred to me anyone would want that many decks. I quickly logged in and added that as an option. The campaign raised $4,341, and the first batch of Climer Cards was printed. With Kickstarter I tested the idea before committing any money. It also was a great publicity tool and I learned a ton. Since then, I have sold thousands of decks of Climer Cards and I consider eight decks a small order. Facilitators and trainers have used them in fifty-seven countries and on all seven continents. In 2023, I released a second deck called Climer Cards 2. I often look back and wonder, "If I had not used Kickstarter, would Climer Cards have been successful?" I doubt it.

Starting small and testing your idea gives you motivation, energy, and priceless information to move forward. In what ways might you test your idea without spending much money or time?

Through the prototype or testing process you will learn more about what needs to be tweaked. From there, you can make the changes and implement at a larger scale.

Action Plans

As you are thinking about how to test or prototype your project, develop a list of action steps required to implement your idea. Continuing with the divergent and convergent theme, start by diverging. List all the action steps you can think of. List them in any order. Just get them in writing. Then converge by sorting them into categories and deciding which ones make sense.

I regularly ask my clients if they have a method of tracking their progress on their projects. Some use a project management tool like Asana, a spreadsheet, or a Google Doc, but many do not have a collective method to track tasks and progress for their collaborative work. I find this concerning.

A team creative process needs to include how you will communicate what each person is working on, their timeline for that task, and what progress they have made. If this only happens verbally, it will slow you down considerably and hamstring your work. Develop a clear, shared action plan that each team member has access to. Determine a process for keeping it up-to-date and spend at least five minutes in each team meeting checking on the group's progress.

Designing and refining your team's creative process is a powerful way to increase your team's deliberate creativity. Following the creative problem solving process and using the tools described here will get your team thinking more creatively together. You now have a solid foundation for deliberate creativity: team purpose, team dynamics, team creative process. Let's look at how to put this all together.

7

From Creative Inspiration to Innovative Integration

F OR OVER a decade I have worked in some way for the North Carolina Outward Bound School. I was a wilderness instructor and led nine-day to twenty-one-day expeditions through the Appalachian Mountains in western North Carolina. Now I am a whitewater canoe instructor and on the board of directors. Outward Bound expeditions involve strenuous backpacking, rock climbing, and whitewater canoeing with groups of twelve students and two instructors. It is not a catered tourist experience with beautiful gourmet meals and luxury accommodations. We eat only after we cook, even if that is at midnight. We sleep under tarps we string up ourselves. If it rains, we only stay dry if we are proactive with rain gear.

When a new group of students arrive, they are wide-eyed and anxious. They only have a vague idea of what to expect. We teach them what they need to know: how to tie knots, how to read a map and use a compass, how to set up a sleeping tarp, how to cook in the woods, how to hang food high up in the trees to keep it safe from bears, and the list goes on.

During the first several days of an expedition, the instructors do a lot of teaching. There are so many new skills the group needs to learn. Without those skills, they will fail. As the group gains competence, the instructors step back, and the group takes on more of a leadership role. By the last portion of the expedition, the instructors are barely needed at all. Some groups even go without their instructors for up to three days because they have become so capable.

We have a saying at Outward Bound that exemplifies the experience—"We are crew, not passengers." It is the individual contribution that brings the team together and makes it whole. It is not about sitting back and waiting for others to step up. It is not about being a passenger on the journey. It is about leaning forward, getting out your compass, and navigating when the crew is lost, even though it would be much easier to sit on a log and complain. Innovation is about engaging in the journey the entire way. Unfortunately, many myths about creativity would tell us the opposite.

For instance, the myth of the eureka moment has prevented countless people from doing the work to be creative. We perpetuate stories that lead us to believe that inspiration will strike us at any second, and we will come up with a brilliant, creative breakthrough that will change the world. Perhaps one of the oldest of these stories is of Sir Isaac Newton discovering gravity.

In 1666, Isaac Newton was sitting under an apple tree. An apple fell out of the tree and hit his head, and he shouted "Eureka!" as he realized gravity exists. He went on to become famous and was knighted by Queen Anne of England. Wow!

Umm—that is not exactly how it happened. By 1666 Newton had been studying math and physics for years, completed his degree at Cambridge University, and had already started developing mathematical theories that led to the formulation of calculus. He did witness an apple fall from a tree, and he did wonder why it fell to the ground and not sideways or up. He thought perhaps there was a force that pulled the apple to the ground. But the apple did not hit his head, there is no proof he shouted "Eureka!" and, most importantly, he did not discover gravity in that one moment. His understanding of gravity took twenty-one years and lots of hard work, dead ends, and divergences. He finally published his findings in 1687 in his book *Principia*, in which he explained the universal laws of motion, including gravity.

There is so much to glean from this story about Newton. First, we tend to be most creative in areas where we have a moderate or deep understanding.[1] I will never generate a brilliant idea about writing computer code or designing couture dresses because these are domains I know almost nothing about.

Second, inspiration is helpful for innovation, but it is just a small part of the process. The hard work that follows inspiration makes something a reality. While ideas might pop in your head when your brain is idle, that eureka moment is only the beginning. And that moment does not count for much. It makes for a great story, but the impressive part is what you and your team do next.

If you ask any prolific writer, artist, musician, or inventor how they can produce creative ideas, they will tell you they just go to work. They sit at the keyboard, pick up a brush, strum chords, or grab their welding torch. They do the work. Writing a book without writing words is difficult, as is writing music without notes. Working through creative problems at work is the same. If you have a problem that needs a creative solution, yet by the end of the day all you have done is respond to 249 emails, you will not have any new ideas for your challenge. Inspiration will not strike, and even if it did, you probably would not notice it.

A Deliberate Creative Team in Action

Let's look at how to integrate the three elements in the system of Deliberate Creative Teams and bring this all together. To review, the three elements are team purpose, team dynamics, and team creative process. If you apply that system, you will produce more creative results. And the good news is you probably do not need to grapple with a challenge for twenty-one years like Newton did. Here's an example of one of my clients whose team embraced the concept of being "crew, not passengers," applied the Deliberate Creative Team System, and impacted millions through a simple software plug-in.

In 2019, Joy Nelson, the president of the Koha Division of ByWater Solutions, enrolled in my Deliberate Creative Team program. The program was a virtual, cohort-based course where leaders learned the Deliberate Creative Team system, with a particular focus on the team creative process. Later that year Joy invited me to work with the Koha development team to teach them the creative problem solving process. Before they started the training, they were trying to be creative, and they were having some success at it. On the Deliberate Creative Spectrum explained in chapter 2, though, the Koha team was sporadic at best. They would fail at times, and they could not figure out why. They did not have a language for or an understanding of the creative process, so from a creativity perspective they could not communicate where they were in a particular project. It was inhibiting their innovation. But knowing their purpose, developing strong team dynamics, and knowing and using a creative process would

We are crew,
not passengers.
**Innovation is
about engaging
in the journey
the entire way.**

prove critical to their success and impact libraries around the world.

ByWater has a unique business model because the product they service is available for free. Koha is an open-source, integrated library system that allows libraries to manage acquisitions, cataloging, circulation, and much more. Libraries that use Koha either have in-house tech support or hire an external service provider, such as ByWater.

A few months after the team finished their Deliberate Creative Team training, the COVID pandemic hit. Someone posted in the Koha online community forum that they would like a Koha plug-in to allow patrons to request curbside pickup. This would eliminate the need to enter the library and would provide a needed service for many. ByWater developers read the request and decided to make the plug-in. Because of the deliberate creativity skills that Joy and her team had been developing, they acted quickly, much more so than some other Koha vendors.

Soon, ByWater released the plug-in for free to libraries around the world. This was a big deal. The innovation meant that millions of people could access their library and get books to learn a new skill, improve their mental health, or just experience the joy of reading. ByWater will never know the total impact that generous change made, but if you enjoy curbside pickup at your local library, it might have been possible because of the innovation and generosity of ByWater Solutions.

Being clear on team purpose meant that when the request for a curbside plug-in came through on the forum, the Koha development team could quickly decide if they wanted to do it. Their primary purpose was to support their library clients to implement Koha, while their secondary purpose was to contribute to the Koha developer community. They looked at their purpose and agreed that the task was an excellent fit. Because Joy and her team had established a common language of creativity through their training, they could talk about the creative process, identifying which of the four phases of creative problem solving they were at and where they wanted to go next.

The team had also been working on improving their team dynamics. As part of the training I did with them, each team member completed the FourSight Thinking System.[2] Four-Sight identifies our preferences for one or more of the four stages of creative problem solving (clarify, ideate, develop, and implement). Joy's team knew that only one team member had a strong preference for developing, so the team tended to jump from ideation to implementation without fully developing solutions. This had created a lot of chaos and extra work. As they clarified their preferences in the creative problem solving process, team members also developed more grace with each other.

Once they understood creative problem solving and each person's FourSight profile, they could approach the innovation in a more streamlined, methodical way. Joy joked that things had become boring. The team was no longer awakened by phone calls in the middle of the night to address an emergency software issue. They did not have fires to put out. Joy said, "My team has a better quality of life, and we are putting out stronger solutions."[3] Their new creativity skills moved them up to the sustainable creative team level on the Deliberate Creative Spectrum. They can consistently be creative and produce innovative results.

When you start focusing on the system of innovation and building your team's skills and strengths in the three areas of team purpose, team dynamics, and team creative process, you will also see an increase in motivation, collaboration, and alignment. Through deliberate action, you will thrive.

How Purpose, Dynamics, and Process Intersect

You have read an example of how one team integrated the three main elements of the Deliberate Creative Team model. Let's go a layer deeper and look at the intersections of these elements, which provide valuable insights into building your team.

THE DELIBERATE CREATIVE TEAM SYSTEM

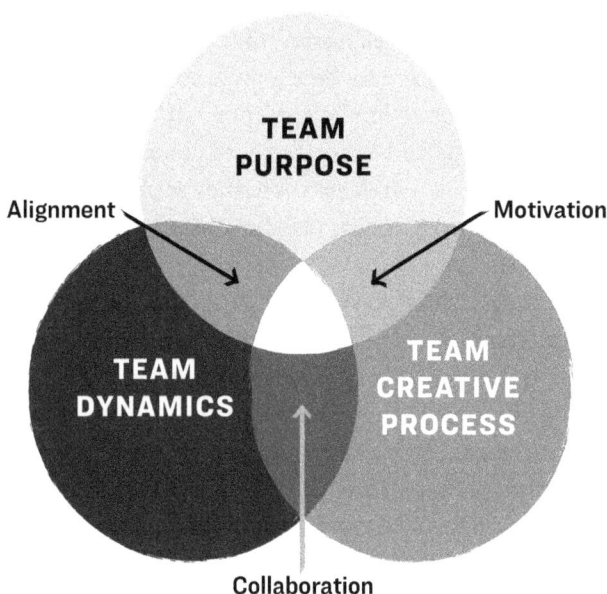

TEAM PURPOSE

Alignment   Motivation

TEAM DYNAMICS   TEAM CREATIVE PROCESS

Collaboration

Motivation

In the Deliberate Creative Team model, the intersection of team purpose and team creative process is motivation. Leaders often ask me about how to motivate their team members to be more creative. They want to create rewards and incentivize innovative results as a tool to motivate employees. The problem is that motivation that comes from rewards is extrinsic and short-lived and does not increase innovation. The attempt at extrinsic motivation in the form of rewards, grades, and prizes risks decreasing intrinsic motivation, which is not what you want. Intrinsic motivation is when a person is driven from within to reach a certain goal or performance metric. It is the most powerful type of motivation. They do whatever they are doing for the satisfaction and joy of it. Creativity requires intrinsic motivation, an internal drive to explore something from a new angle, to generate ideas, to develop those ideas into a viable solution, and then to implement experiments to see what works.

While they can have limited use, rewards like cash bonuses, innovation competitions, and stock options generally do not drive innovation. They are usually individually focused, and their competitive nature can inadvertently spur poor team behavior, decreasing creativity.

Rewards are a fancy version of the carrot-and-stick approach. They are what Daniel Pink, author of *Drive*, calls Motivation 2.0. (He uses 2.0 because Motivation 1.0 is based on mere survival instincts.) But today, we are evolving past the carrot and stick into Motivation 3.0. Pink identifies that a sense of purpose, autonomy, and mastery are the primary drivers of intrinsic motivation.[4] These align well with being creative. If you have a clear sense of purpose, the autonomy to do the work, and the opportunity for improving skills (mastery), you will remain intrinsically motivated. In most cases, these factors are not hard to set up for teams. If you are following the Deliberate Creative Team system, these will likely fall into place.

There might be one exception to rewards negatively influencing creativity. If you pair rewards with creativity training, you might get more creative results. Some experiments have shown this in short-term, controlled environments. For instance, in a study led by James Burroughs at the University of Virginia, engineering students were challenged with the task of designing a car jack for people over sixty years old.[5] Half the students received a short lesson on creative techniques. The other half did not receive any training. Researchers also told half of each group that the top three most creative solutions would be rewarded with $250, $100, and $50 cash prizes. For the group that did not get any training, the reward incentive had a slightly negative impact on their creativity. For those who did get the training, the reward seemed to increase their creativity slightly, although whether this was attributable to extrinsic or intrinsic motivation was unclear.

The one benefit of rewards and awards is that they can send an important message about organizational values. In 2016, shortly after I finished my dissertation research on Deliberate Creative Teams, I received the Karl Rohnke Creativity Award from the Association for Experiential Education. I had been part of this association for my entire career and the members knew my work on creativity, including the creative products I designed, such as Climer Cards and the trainings and workshops I developed. When I got the phone call that I was being recognized with this award, I was completely surprised. I was not producing creative work in hopes of getting this award. After receiving it I was not driven to be more creative. But the award communicated to me and others that this association values creativity enough to recognize it publicly. They want to see more creativity in the field of experiential education. For me, it created a sense of connection and trust with the association. That in turn may drive me to take more risks with creative ideas, at least with this audience.

Awards and rewards can be positive, but they are unlikely to increase creativity or inspire your team to generate new ideas. Rather than putting money into rewards alone, you will see greater results by providing creativity training or combining rewards with training. Plus, a more powerful tool to motivate employees creates a positive loop toward innovative work.

Teresa Amabile from the Harvard Business School and psychologist Steven Kramer designed an impressive study that analyzed nearly twelve thousand journal entries from 238 team members in twenty-six teams at seven companies. At the end of each day, team members were asked to answer several short questions about the day. The most important question was "Briefly describe one event from today that stands out in your mind."

After compiling data for months, Amabile and her team analyzed the results. She found what she calls the progress principle. Making small, frequent wins on projects or tasks leads to a rich, positive inner work life. An inner work life is the "mostly invisible parts of each individual's experience— the thoughts, feelings, and drives triggered by the events of the day."[6] A rich inner work life leads to more creativity and productivity. It motivates us to do even more. This is the heart of intrinsic motivation.

If you do want to create awards or rewards, keep them light, positive, and focused on elevating the value of innovation. People find joy and satisfaction in doing what they are good at. So, to increase your team's motivation to innovate, clarify your team's purpose, invest in creativity training, and develop strong creative processes. Your team members will increase their skills and find the creative process more meaningful and rewarding.

Collaboration

In the Deliberate Creative Team system, the overlap of team dynamics and team creative process leads to collaboration. We briefly explored collaboration in chapter 3 when comparing cooperation and collaboration. When team members collaborate, they meld their intellect and skills to collectively create something new. The hardest part of collaboration is that it requires each individual to have a reasonable amount of interpersonal skills. As you develop your team dynamics and use intentional processes to be more creative, you will increase your team's ability to collaborate.

Several years ago my friends Mary and Kiera called me and said that Amy Ray was playing in town that night. That evening I drove five minutes down the road to Isis Music Hall and watched a beautiful creative collaboration unfold. Amy Ray is one-half of the famed Grammy-winning Indigo Girls. I have been a fan of the Indigo Girls since college, and one of the treats of living in Asheville, North Carolina, is that Amy Ray plays here frequently. The more I see her perform live, the more of a fan I become. She clearly thinks deeply about her craft and has honed the process of creative collaboration.

The venue was small and not too crowded, so we stood about ten feet from the stage. My favorite part of the show was watching the band interact with each other. They would look at each other mid-song and communicate a lot with an eyebrow raise, half smile, or head nod. They were so tuned in to each other. It was obvious they had great team dynamics and had worked through the creative process many times to get to such a high level of collaboration.

During his opening set, Phil Cook spoke about working with Amy Ray. He talked about producing her album *Goodnight Tender* and how they elevated each other by pushing each other creatively. As he performed the opening set, Amy was standing in the wings watching him with a small smile on her face. Then as Amy Ray and her band performed, I saw Phil was on the side, admiring her set. He eventually joined her on stage for a song or two. There was a chemistry between them, not of a romantic nature but a creative buzz that felt electric.

Start by applying your new creativity skills to **something simple.**

Something that has always impressed me about musical collaboration is the back-and-forth, iterative nature of it, especially when writing a song or during improv jam sessions. One person plays a riff, another adds to it, a third produces another variation. No one says, "Oh, that will never work!" Everyone knows that they are experimenting and that something cool might emerge. More teams would benefit from embodying this kind of collective ethos, from bringing the spirit of musical collaboration into the conference room.

What I saw in Amy Ray, her band, and her producer Phil Cook was a team who had developed a deep level of trust and psychological safety, who knew how to engage in creative abrasion, and who communicated well—all the ingredients for strong team dynamics. They also had honed their creative process. They knew how to clarify the challenge, generate new ideas, develop them further, and implement them. The result was a creative collaboration of a team who has connected with hundreds of thousands through millions of musical notes.

Alignment

When teams have a clear purpose and strong team dynamics, they reach a creative alignment that drives their motivation and increases collaboration. As you get clear on your team purpose through shared goals, your team members will feel more committed to the team. That commitment also increases as the team dynamics improve. We are going to be more committed to a team if we feel good about being around them. When we feel psychologically safe, we feel more connected and that also leads to greater alignment.

In 2024, I was invited to emcee TEDxAsheville for the second time. I love it when I emcee an event more than once because I get to build on the previous experience and make it even better. On a chilly January day two months before the event, I met with Barrie Barton, the lead coordinator, and Vanessa Bell, the strategy advisor. Sitting in a café booth, we mapped out how the event would flow. The speaker order had already been determined, but we were working on how to engage the audience throughout the full day, the transitions between speakers, and integrating the dance troupe that would be performing after lunch. Essentially, planning the aspects that I would be leading from stage.

Lots of the ideas in that meeting were scrapped, but the few that survived indicated we had a clear sense of purpose. We had talked many times about our vision for the event. We wanted it to go beyond an audience listening to speakers. Sitting and listening to speakers for five to six hours is a long time! We wanted the nearly five hundred attendees to interact with one another and be engaged. We wanted them to feel a sense of connection to each other, to TEDx, and to our broader Asheville community. I could envision the energy I wanted in the audience.

Barrie, Vanessa, and I also had a solid sense of team dynamics. We had known each other for several years; we worked together during the previous TEDx. Our relationship went beyond volunteering for TEDx. Vanessa, a graphic designer, had designed two logos for me, and Barrie had been a coaching client of mine. Vanessa and Barrie had worked closely together on leading two TEDx events and many smaller events. Our team dynamics were solid. We all felt comfortable enough to throw ideas onto the table and to dissect, rearrange, elevate, or discard those ideas.

Our clear sense of purpose and strong team dynamics led to creative alignment. The end result was a stellar event! Two days after TEDx, I was standing in a hardware store staring at light bulbs. A couple walked down the same aisle and one of them abruptly stopped near me. I turned to look at her, and she said, "Didn't you emcee TEDx on Friday?"

I chuckled. "Yes, I did. Were you there?"

"Yes! I loved it!" She continued to tell me that a highlight for her was the conversation she had at lunch. Because of the directions I had given before lunch, she had an amazing conversation with someone she did not know before the event. They explored the morning's talks and made a valuable connection with each other. Ah! Mission accomplished! I was so happy to hear that the way we designed and facilitated the event allowed people to make true connections, even in a room of five hundred attendees. One of our main goals had been met. That is creative alignment at work.

AS A LEADER, when you intentionally lead your team to develop a clear purpose, set the conditions for strong team dynamics, and facilitate the creative process, your team will experience motivation, collaboration, and alignment. This, in turn, leads to innovative results.

This is the Deliberate Creative Team system. Enacting the system requires team members to develop skills and competencies along the way. As they grow together, the system becomes a framework, a methodology, and an approach. The system takes what at first seems like a nebulous process reserved for a few with the "creative gene" and turns it into an explicit, clear approach the team can follow to be more creative.

Activity: Develop Team Working Agreements

Purpose: to explicitly develop group norms

Time: thirty to sixty minutes

Materials: markers, flipchart paper

While you are leading your team to be more creative, a great technique to deepen alignment and strengthen collaboration is to develop a set of team working agreements. This will help your team be ready to tackle the inevitable barriers to creativity.

Over time, every team develops norms. Norms are the typical ways the team interacts with each other. They emerge whether the team is intentional about developing them or not. For instance, whether team meetings always start right on time or a few minutes late is a norm. The challenge is that most teams have not been explicit about developing the norms and sometimes unwanted norms evolve.

Developing a list of team norms or working agreements makes the implicit explicit. It fosters psychological safety and a sense of inclusion. It eliminates some confusion around expectations. Working agreements are a list of behaviors that say, "This is how we agree to work together."

A few working agreements from one of my clients are:

- Lead with compassion.
- Be open and honest with each other.
- Engage in respectful disagreement (e.g., task conflict).
- Be yourself and support others in being themselves.

To start, explain the purpose of working agreements and the value of creating them together. Give the group some quiet time to think about the following prompt and jot down their thoughts: "Imagine our team one year from now. We are working well together and collaborating at a high level. We have developed into a Deliberate Creative Team. Quietly write down a few behaviors that team members engage in with each other that help us work well together."

After a few minutes when it looks like each person has two or three thoughts written down, invite team members to share their thoughts out loud. Scribe the responses on a flipchart. Develop a collaborative list and then edit them into working agreements. Invite the group to do a little wordsmithing to make each agreement work well. Scratch off words, consolidate, or delete anything that the group feels they do not need. I think it is best to keep the list relatively short, ideally less than ten items. I also suggest starting each agreement with a verb. Make sure each item is clear enough that it will make sense in the future, not just in the context of the moment.

Once the list is complete, ensure everyone feels good about striving toward the agreements. The expectation is not perfection, but that the team knows what they are working toward together. It is inevitable that someone will break one of the agreements. We are human. We mess up. Discuss what the team wants to do when someone breaks an agreement. How will it be addressed? How will repairs or restoration be made? Sometimes I invite everyone to sign their name on the flipchart to show commitment to the team's working agreements.

After the working agreements are created, keep them visible during team meetings. Some teams hang up the flipchart; others list them at the bottom of each agenda. One of my clients printed little cards that each person brings to the team meetings as a reminder for themselves.

8

How to Clear the Path for Creativity

N OW THAT YOU have an understanding of the Deliberate Creative Team system, let's look at what gets in the way of innovation. There are many barriers to being creative. These include lack of time, scarcity of resources, a discouraging company culture, and limited internal beliefs. As a leader, you want your team to eliminate these barriers. Let's look at each of these in more depth.

Find the Time

For many people, one of the biggest barriers to being creative is time. Creativity takes time, and most of us need more of it. Or do we? We all get the same amount of time in a day, you know that. The difference is what we do with it. I have noticed from working with my clients that there are two big challenges with time.

The first is an organization using outdated processes and procedures that could be streamlined to free up more time.

The second is that as people begin new initiatives and new processes, they do not let go of the old ones. Staff feel overwhelmed with the volume of work and do not want to try anything new because that will just increase their workload. Let's look at how to make changes so you and your team can be freed up to be more innovative.

Antiquated Bureaucratic Remnants

If your company has been around for more than a decade, it likely has something I call antiquated bureaucratic remnants impeding its innovation.

I was hired by a city municipality to facilitate a two-day retreat for the city council. I was five weeks into the eight-week engagement and we still did not have the contract signed. Before the project began, I sent them my contract, but they wanted to use their own. I reviewed their contract and told them it looked good. Weeks later they emailed me the final version. I immediately signed it and emailed it back. Then I got this response: "Hi Amy, on the page you signed, we also need it to be notarized."

Notarized? You have got to be kidding me. This was 2024. I have worked with the US Department of Defense, the US Department of Homeland Security, and other federal agencies. I have worked for state governments, local municipalities, universities, and large and small for-profit companies. This request for notarization was a first. We had been in multiple meetings together on Zoom, one of their lead staff had met me at least three times in person, and six months earlier as an emcee, I had introduced the mayor at a conference. They had plenty of evidence that I was who I said I was.

Getting this notarized meant extra work for me. The main deliverable for this client (the two-day retreat) was the following week and I still had a lot of prep to do, including creative ideas that would take time to implement. I also had other clients and other commitments. Now they were saying I had to find a notary, in person, and get this contract signed. This felt like pointless busywork and was getting in the way of my innovating.

I responded to their email and pushed back a bit. The prior year, I had signed a contract for a different engagement with them. No notary was needed then. Why now? Was this really necessary? Their email back to me said, "I know it seems outdated, but unfortunately it is part of our process."

I decided I would take care of it in a few days. Then in a positive, unexpected spin, they called me the next day and verbally confirmed that I had signed the contract. That was a relief. No notary was needed. I was grateful for their change of heart.

This initial requirement is what I call an antiquated bureaucratic remnant. That is, a process, procedure, or rule created in the distant past that no longer meets the initial purpose but is woven into the organization in a way that no one questions. All processes, procedures, and rules in any company were created by people, most likely by employees who work at that organization. That means they can be changed, updated, or eliminated by employees. What processes, procedures, or rules does your organization have that feel like busywork and impede innovation? They likely fall into the category of travel reimbursements, certain reports, or anything with the word "requisition" in it.

Likely there was a time in the distant past when the procedure was necessary. Yet no one even remembers what the purpose of the procedure is. These remnants are a waste of time, money, and energy that could be spent on more valuable, innovative work. Perhaps you still need to gather the information, but it could be done more efficiently. For instance, anything that requires printing a PDF and sending a signed physical copy through interoffice mail is likely outdated. Change that to an online form with an electronic signature. Do you require a physical receipt to be turned in with travel forms? If I can deposit a five-figure check to my bank with a photo, your company does not need a physical receipt for a coffee from Starbucks. A digital one will do.

I have left more than one job because I could not stand the outdated processes, procedures, or rules that were impeding real progress, real work that would make a difference in people's lives. I have seen countless highly intelligent, creative people waste time and energy on antiquated bureaucratic remnants. I have seen good ideas thrown out because employees did not want to deal with the bureaucracy, whether it was getting approval or filling out paperwork. Often clients say to me, "Amy, we can't do that. Do you know how much paperwork it would take?" They always sound so dejected. My heart breaks a little when I hear this.

I get checks and balances. To be clear, that is not what I am talking about. Many processes, procedures, and rules are valuable and worthwhile. I am talking about outdated systems that have not changed for years and are no longer serving their original purpose. If you have an employee who has been working at your company for thirty years, ask them if they remember how long a certain system has been in place. If they say, "That's how it's been as long as I've been here," you may have an antiquated bureaucratic remnant on your hands.

Do your employees and clients a favor and update your procedures to be efficient and eliminate those that are no longer needed. A great approach to making this change is to use the creative problem solving process to clarify the issue, generate new ideas, develop them into solutions, and finally implement the new changes. And for everyone's sanity, please use modern technology.

Budget for Innovation

I cannot tell you how many times in my career I have heard the phrase "We can't do that because it's not in our budget." Of course it is not in your budget. Innovation is never in the budget. Budgets are built around last year's ideas, last year's situation, and last year's plan. You cannot be innovative if you stick to the budget. Do yourself a favor and next time you write a budget, include a line item for new ideas. You cannot predict what is coming up, but you can budget for the unexpected idea.

A few years ago, one of my recurring nonprofit clients called me and asked me to facilitate a deliberate creativity session with their board. The organization's director of operations explained that they try to build flexibility into their budget for needs that arise during the year and usually have a line item in their budget for miscellaneous ideas and outside consults. This particular year, when the finances were a bit tighter, they had deleted that budget line and she was feeling the loss. She could not move forward with some new ideas, and she felt stuck. As we talked through the options given her limited budget, she said, "Budget for innovation. It costs money. It's an investment." The opportunity to innovate is, in part, what has kept her with the organization for eight years. The excitement of new initiatives drives the organization toward its vision, keeping her and other employees engaged and motivated. The following year, the line item for new ideas was back in their budget.

What might happen if you added a line item called "innovative ideas," "unexpected innovation," or "creative exploration"? Set aside a small amount and see what comes up. This might be $500, $5,000, or $50,000 depending on your overall budget. Perhaps something evolves that then becomes a

Budget for
innovation.

significant income stream, improves an inefficiency, or leads to an important change. The possibilities are truly endless. But the ideas will end quickly if you cannot move forward with at least some of them. Budget for innovation.

And what do you do today if you have not budgeted for innovation? In chapter 6 I mentioned an activity called PPCO. The *C* and *O* stand for "concerns" and "overcoming concerns." Some typical concerns with most ideas are "It is too expensive," "We cannot afford it," or "The board won't approve it." Overcoming the concerns means looking at the problem differently. Create a few "How might we…" questions to generate new ideas. For instance, "How might we implement this in a way that costs less than $500?" Or "How might we find a funder to underwrite the cost of this idea?" Work together to answer the question. How many ideas can you come up with? I find that answering these financial questions is a particularly great time to bring in that second divergent thinking rule—get wild and wacky.

Remember the ALS Ice Bucket Challenge? Three men with ALS—Anthony Senerchia, Pete Frates, and Pat Quinn—inspired seventeen million people to video themselves dumping a bucket of ice water on their head, post it on social media, and donate to ALS.[1] The ALS Association raised $115 million, and ten years later they are still spending that money.

If you cannot raise money, how might you implement your idea on a shoestring budget? How might you prototype with a 3D printer? How might you get students from a local college to help you in exchange for class credit? How might you implement on a tiny scale to start?

Measure What Matters

You want to measure what matters. When teams number their ideas, they generate more ideas.[2] Since having more ideas leads to better ideas, numbering them makes sense.[3] When you first start ideating with a team, aim for a certain number of new ideas. Depending on how much time you have, start low, maybe thirty-five or fifty ideas. As you gain more experience or if you have more time, aim for one hundred or more. The numbers provide a fun goal to work toward too. If you have forty-three ideas and you need to get to fifty, those last seven can be really fun. Numbering the ideas increases motivation and pushes the team to produce more novel, unique ideas.

Be careful that you are measuring what you actually care about. A client of mine is in a brand-new role as vice president of operations for a software company. She told me about an unusual metric at her new company. The customer success team is required to track the number of emails they send each month. To be considered successful they need to send two hundred or more emails per month. As a new VP, she has attempted to discuss the idea of quality of emails over quantity with the leadership, but they are not budging. I was completely flummoxed and asked, "What is the reason they want you to send two hundred emails a month?"

She said, "Emails are what they've always tracked. 'There's a place for it in the dashboard. See? It's important.' In the mind of leadership more emails equals better performance. In fact, they will be letting someone go from the company who doesn't hit this KPI. As you probably guessed, she is really good at her job and usually writes a longer single message instead of ten short ones."

To meet this pointless metric, some employees write thank-you emails in response to thank-you emails. Seriously. I did not make this up. It is a great example of the unintended consequence of measuring the wrong thing. People are smart and adaptable. They will find a way to work within the systems set up, however odd and pointless they seem. You just might not get the results you hoped for.

Directly measure what matters. Stop measuring trivial things that don't matter. Sometimes measuring the outcome directly is hard and you want something more immediate. If the quantity of emails led to better customer service, then this measurement would make sense. Take some time to dig into what matters and measure that thing. For instance, if quality of customer service matters, then perhaps use customer satisfaction surveys, measure the percentage of customers who return to do business again, or check how speedily customers' issues are resolved. Measuring what matters will lead to more positive, creative results and eliminate the busywork that impedes creativity.

Abandon the Status Quo

Company cultures influence the innovation of teams. If a culture discourages innovation, then teams are not going to pursue it. In *The Culture Code*, Daniel Coyle writes about interviewing Ed Catmull, the former president and cofounder of Pixar and the coleader of Disney Animation Studios.[4] Catmull talks about the importance of setting up systems to support innovation. Part of this means dismantling systems that get in the way of the creative work.

It takes a little rebelliousness to be creative. Creativity is about abandoning the status quo. It is about letting go of some people's favorite phrase, "We have always done it this way." If those seven words are like a sword to your heart and cause pain deep in your belly, then you are rebellious enough to be creative. The challenge is you have to push back against

"If it ain't broke, don't fix it." Some people cannot tell it is broken. The process is so ingrained in their head that they no longer notice it takes fifteen steps instead of three. For instance, it never occurred to them they could save time by sending a PDF instead of mailing an invoice. You laugh, but it is a true story.

In 2011 I was hired by our local recreation department to develop a challenge course and team-building program for area businesses. My work was only part-time; I worked from home and went into the office a couple of times each month. About six weeks into my job, I was in the office and found out I had an office mailbox. To my surprise I had mail. Underneath a yellow flyer about a local 5k run was an unsealed, unmailed envelope addressed to one of our new clients. Inside was an invoice. I took this to my supervisor and asked why it was in my mailbox. I assumed it was a copy for my records but wanted to make sure. She told me to go ask Donna, who processed the invoices.

I walked down the hall to see Donna. I knocked on her open cubicle space, and she swiveled around in her office chair. Behind her were stacked plastic trays stuffed with papers, the original inbox. On her cubicle walls hung assorted memos, crayon drawings, and photos of her grandkids. I reintroduced myself since we had only met once. I showed her the envelope and asked her if this was a copy of the invoice sent to the client.

She said, "No. I print out the invoice and put it in your mailbox. Then you mail it out to the client."

Now I was really confused. "You mean you don't mail the invoice? I need to manually do that myself?"

"Yes."

I looked down at the invoice. It was a month old. I now understood why our new clients were taking so long to pay. They didn't have an invoice! I knew I could not come into the office every time an invoice was ready just to put a stamp on an envelope and put it in the mail slot. In addition to this job, I also had a consulting business.

I explained to Donna that I did not work in the office and did not even have a desk. I asked her, "We do not have many clients for the challenge course program. Would it be possible for you to stamp and mail the invoices for me?"

"No. I can't do that. I send out sixteen thousand invoices each year and book the gyms and community spaces for the whole city."

My jaw dropped. Sixteen thousand invoices were being manually processed through postal mail each year! This was a nonprofit. The paper, envelopes, and postage had to cost nearly $1 per invoice. If we could do this digitally, we could save up to $16,000 per year. Plus, we would get paid quicker and spend less time trying to track down payments.

"The clients I work with are comfortable with email and would prefer to get the invoice as a PDF. Instead of printing my invoices, could you send me the PDF and I could email it to them?" I thought this would be an easy solution and she would quickly agree.

Instead, she shifted a bit in her seat and started to look uncomfortable. "No. I can't do that. The computer program I use doesn't create PDFs."

I almost started laughing. I had no idea what program she used, but if a program will print, it can produce a PDF. I explained this, but she insisted it would not work. After a few more minutes of conversation, I finally said, "Donna, do you know what a PDF is?"

She hesitated and said, "Yeah, it's something you get in an email."

Oh my. This was a much bigger problem than I realized. She did not fully understand what a PDF was, and her computer skills were lower than I realized. She could process her job exactly as taught, but she was not going to problem-solve with me. I politely thanked her and left.

I walked back down the hall to my supervisor's office. I plopped down in the empty chair by her desk. She saw the bewildered look on my face and said, "That bad, huh?" She had worked in the department for years, and I had a feeling she knew exactly what I had just experienced.

I relayed the conversation to her, and she just shook her head. Then she told me to go talk to the accountant who supervises Donna. I walked down a different hallway to his office and introduced myself. I explained that I needed a way to quickly send invoices to clients that did not require me to drive across town to put a stamp on an envelope. I also understood that my little team-building program was a small cog in this bigger organization that served thousands of people each year. It seemed to me this was an opportunity to look at making a small change to save time and money across the entire organization.

It became clear, though, that no one wanted to talk with Donna about making this change.

The accountant was a kind, quiet man who decided that anytime I needed an invoice, he would go into the program and create a PDF of the invoice Donna generated and email it to me. I thought this was a ridiculous use of his time, but he said he was happy to do it. Perhaps he was happy because it meant he did not have to talk with Donna about changing the process. I walked back down the hall and told Donna of the new solution. She no longer needed to print my invoices.

My small problem was solved and things worked well for the next two years I was in that role. However, the situation always bothered me. Had I been full-time and more invested in the whole organization, I would have worked harder to

It takes a little
**rebelliousness
to be creative.**

lead this change and help the organization use technology to save money and improve processes. The situation was a great example that barriers to innovation are rarely about a lack of ideas. The barriers are much deeper.

On one hand, this was an antiquated bureaucratic remnant, but it was more than that. Despite what it may have looked like on the surface, this was not a simple technical problem. It involved human emotions and biology, and those almost always make situations more complex. This required an adaptive approach.

Set Up for Successful Change

Technical problems are characterized by clear cause-and-effect relationships that are easily recognized. They require straightforward management approaches where tasks can be easily delegated. There are known solutions and you apply those solutions to make the fix: The copy machine breaks, and you call in the technician to fix it. You can also draw upon best practices from other teams or organizations.

Adaptive problems resist simple technical solutions because they require a change in human behavior. They may require individuals to shift their identity, learn new skills, or let go of old habits. They are much harder than technical changes. Harvard professors and leadership experts Ronald Heifetz, Alexander Grashow, and Marty Linsky coauthored the book *The Practice of Adaptive Leadership*.[5] They point out that one of the biggest errors that leaders make is they address an adaptive problem with a technical solution. It happens all the time.

Let's take the situation with Donna and the invoices. Imagine you are the leader of that organization. If you approach the situation as a technical problem, then you might announce at a staff meeting that from now on all invoices will be emailed as PDFs and not mailed. Maybe you would tell Donna in advance, or maybe not. The way you see it, it is just a matter of changing a few steps in a process. Easy.

Next thing you know, Donna is freaking out. Other staff are backing her up and telling you this change is ridiculous and unnecessary. You are shocked at the resistance. Two days later you are in a meeting with Donna's union rep and being told you cannot make this change. You never saw this resistance coming.

Now, let's imagine you approach this as the adaptive problem it actually is. You recognize that this may be a tough change for Donna. She has been a faithful employee for years and you know that she likes the predictability and consistency of her job. You are aware that if you spring this change on her, she might feel her sense of autonomy is threatened because she has no control over events. She might be scared because she does not know how to create a PDF and she fears she might lose her job. Her sense of certainty feels threatened. But you could approach this change in a way that decreases the sense of threat Donna might feel.

You set up the meeting with her. You tell her you want to make a change and save the organization money and provide better service to customers. She is a critical part of this change and you need her help. You gradually get some buy-in from her on the importance of this change. You also agree to provide her with lots of support to learn how to process PDFs and approach her work in a new way. You ask her what other changes she thinks are needed throughout the organization so that this goes smoothly. Throughout the whole experience, you work hard to ensure Donna feels a sense of psychological safety and purpose. The more collaborative you can make the process, the better. Within a few months, all invoices are being processed digitally and the organization is saving thousands of dollars. At a future staff meeting, you recognize Donna for all her hard work and for being a critical part of making the organization better.

As frustrating as it may be to experience resistance to change, the reason is directly related to our biology.

In the last couple of decades, neuroscience has discovered that humans react to perceived social threats in the same way we react to threats to physical survival. This speaks to how important community and collaboration are for us as a species. It also explains why sometimes we have outsized reactions to new ideas or a colleague's comment. We feel threatened socially and probably do not even realize it. In 2008, David Rock developed the SCARF model, which categorizes the five domains of social experience and sheds light on why we act the way we do.[6] Here are the five domains:

1   **Status:** Our relative importance to others, personal worth

2   **Certainty:** Being able to predict the future

3   **Autonomy:** Our sense of control over events

4   **Relatedness:** Our sense of safety around others, a sense of connection

5   **Fairness:** Our perception of fair exchanges between people

When in social situations, like at work, each of us reacts by perceiving if we are threatened or rewarded in each of these areas. This is deeply subconscious; often we do not realize what is happening. As a leader, when you want to lead a change, you need to assess if others will be threatened in any of these areas. Then you decide if you need to approach the problem as an adaptive or technical problem. If you can get that part of the approach right, your change efforts will be much more successful.

Take Risks

Clients often ask me how they can be sure a new idea will work. My answer is "You can't." That is the challenge with doing something new. It has not been done before (at least in this context) so you cannot know if it will work. Be willing to take the risk and try. Organizations that have a culture where failure is acceptable, and even encouraged, tend to also foster the most innovation. You want to set up systems and opportunities where failure is okay.

When you understand creativity and how to innovate on demand, you can apply your knowledge, skills, and abilities and get creative. A few years ago, I had an unexpected opportunity to take a risk and I realized all my creative skills were going to be put to the test.

I have been leading webinars and virtual programs since at least 2016. Years later, when COVID hit and suddenly everyone wanted to switch over to virtual meetings, many colleagues and friends asked me to teach them how to be more engaging on Zoom. At first, I was happy to help. But after opening the fifteenth email with a question about Zoom, I said out loud to my empty office, "What am I, a Zoom expert or something?"

Then I just started laughing at myself. Given that I had been using Zoom and similar tools for years, I supposed that compared to most people I was an expert. I realized I had some important skills others needed to learn.

I decided to offer a free webinar to teach people some of the skills they needed to lead online meetings. To my surprise, six hundred people enrolled and at least half of them I did not know. At the end of the webinar, I announced a new class called Leading Engaging Virtual Meetings. I remember feeling so nervous. Would anyone even care about the class? What if no one signed up? But I knew it didn't matter. Failure

In an urgent situation, you will thrive if you already know how to be innovative.

was an option, and to be creative I had to take the risk, put myself out there, and see what happened.

Fortunately, it was not a failure. Over the next year, I taught hundreds of facilitators and trainers how to lead meaningful virtual sessions. Financially, it was my best year up to that point. Plus, I had a blast connecting with people from around the world in ways I never would have otherwise. When I look back on that year, I realize my success was because of my ability to be deliberately creative. I understood how creativity works. I could intentionally use that to design, develop, and launch a new program that positively improved so many lives.

I used the creative problem solving process as I developed the new course, engaged with my audience in new ways, and helped hundreds of people. I started with the clarify stage. What did my students need to learn? What were they struggling with? What was the best way to teach them? I tried to look at what they already knew, what they needed to know, and what I could teach them. I talked with potential students to find out where they were stuck. I sought out perspectives from colleagues with similar experience to me. How might I design an amazing course that teaches professionals how to lead engaging virtual meetings and trainings?

From there I moved into the ideate stage. I generated lots of ideas of what to include in the course. I also examined different formats—is a synchronous live program better than prerecorded videos? I stayed in the divergent thinking mode before converging on the best ideas. I then took the best ideas into the develop stage.

In the develop stage I mapped out the course and got organized. What was the best order of the videos? How should they be grouped? It was in this stage that I ended up developing a conceptual model explaining what they needed to know to lead engaging virtual sessions.

Finally, I got to the implement stage. I recorded videos, designed handouts, wrote the website copy, and created the course.

I dreamed up this course and launched it in less than one month. I navigated around roadblocks that came up, brushed aside the naysayers (both internal and external), and got the important work done. Over the following year I taught hundreds of professionals how to design and lead more engaging virtual meetings. It felt good and I was proud of the work I did that year.

You never know when you will need to be creative with little notice. When you do, you will thrive if you already know how to be innovative. In an urgent situation, it is too late to learn. When someone you are with needs lifesaving CPR, you are in no position to learn the techniques. You need to already know how to provide rescue breathing and chest compressions because you need to act immediately.

Alone and Together

Years ago, I had the privilege to interview Mihaly Csikszentmihalyi. The late researcher was a pioneer in the field of creativity. In addition to discovering flow, he created the field of positive psychology with Martin Seligman.

I asked Csikszentmihalyi to speak about his experience with teams and what he saw as the intersection between teams and creativity. He said there is an interesting tug on the creative person. They need to balance their extroversion and introversion. They need to explore ideas with other people and to further their thinking about a specific topic. Then they need to go back and spend quiet time thinking and working to further develop those ideas. The ebb and flow between alone time and people time and the wavelengths between the ebb and flow can vary. Someone could spend three or four months being extroverted and talking with people, then just as long thinking, writing, and exploring their questions on their own.

Or it could happen daily, such as for the CEO of a large banking corporation. During our interview, Csikszentmihalyi explained that each day the CEO would "close his office door at 7:30 a.m. ... until 10:30 a.m. For three hours no matter what happened he couldn't be disturbed. His secretary would screen all the calls."[7] During that time he would figure out his priorities, generate new ideas, and solve current problems. Then at 10:30 a.m., he would open the door and begin working with his vice presidents and staff. He was balancing the rhythm of introversion and extroversion.

In his book *Creativity*, Csikszentmihalyi also states: "Creative people seem to harbor opposite tendencies on the continuum between extroversion and introversion. Usually, each of us tends to be one or the other, either preferring to be in the thick of crowds or sitting on the sidelines and observing the passing show... Creative individuals, on the other hand, seem to express both traits at the same time."[8]

For creativity to flourish, we need to balance time with others and time alone. Sometimes this can be hard when we work in a busy office with lots of people. Often in science labs, the understanding is that when someone is wearing latex gloves you do not bother them. The gloves provide a cue to colleagues; much like the pattern of the CEO above, a clear cue can be a valuable way to get that important quiet time needed to develop creative ideas.

When the open-office concept became popular, Widen (now Acquia DAM) redesigned their space so that everyone in the company had a desk in a big open space. While this made it easy to chat with colleagues and skip an email for a simple question, it also meant employees were continually being interrupted and it was hard to do deeper, more focused work.

I worked with one of the Widen teams to apply the creative problem solving process to their challenge. Within a couple of hours, we had a new solution. They created little signs that mimicked a traffic light. Each person had one at their desk and they could decide to put out a red, yellow, or green signal. Green meant "you are welcome to interrupt me." Yellow meant "I am trying to focus, but if it is important you can interrupt." Red meant "only interrupt me in case of an emergency." It worked well. The new system enabled them to balance their quiet time and their collaborative time. No matter how extroverted someone is, they still need quiet time to do deeper work. Ask yourself, What structures are in place to foster both group work and individual work? What changes to the physical space or the organization's expectations and culture can be adjusted to foster the balance?

Expose Limiting Internal Beliefs

On my first day of school for my PhD program at Antioch University, I gathered in a room of twenty-five other students. There was a lot of handshaking and introductions and a nervous excitement in the air. Once we were settled in our seats, the dean and program chair, Laurien Alexandre, welcomed us. Within the first ten minutes she said she wanted to address the elephant in the room.

Before the orientation, we had all received bios of the twenty-five members in our cohort. They were impressive, although admittedly I was so overwhelmed with the large volume of books we were required to read that I had not paid much attention to the bios. Alexandre commented that our group included a dean at a college in New York, vice presidents of big companies, an emergency room nurse working in one of the busiest hospitals in Canada, and a US Representative who ran for president of the United States on the Green Party ticket.

Wait, what? US president! I was not that nervous before, but now my brow was furrowing. I was trying to remain cool.

Alexandre added that some of us might be wondering why we had been accepted into the program. She assured us that Antioch did not make a mistake. Our application did not slip through the cracks. We were all there because the faculty knew we had what it takes to succeed.

Wow. A far cry from the first day of organic chemistry, when the professor rattled out the old cliché, "Look to your left. Look to your right. One of you will fail this class."

Alexandre told us about imposter syndrome. I had never heard of it, but I had definitely experienced it. Imposter syndrome is also known as the troll, the inner critic, the monster in your head, or the devil on your shoulder. It is the voice in your head that says you cannot do it, you are not good enough, other people are smarter, better, more beautiful... insert adjective of your choosing.

If right now you are telling yourself you do not have a voice in your head, that's the voice. Nearly all of us have it.

In her book *Waking Up to Your Worth*, Jennifer Wilson explains that imposter syndrome affects people from all genders, races, ages, demographic backgrounds—essentially from all walks of life.[9]

When you experience imposter syndrome, your past achievements are more or less irrelevant. Oprah said that of the 37,000 people she has interviewed, they all asked the same question after the interview: "How did I do? Was that okay?" From criminals being interviewed in prison to accomplished professionals, every person wanted to know they did well and they were heard. Even Barack Obama and Beyoncé asked it![10]

Alexandre is a brilliant leader. Her wisdom in sharing about imposter syndrome on our first day of school led to a collective deep breath. We relaxed a bit. We shook off those first-day jitters. My cohort met often over the next three years, and we talked about that moment many times. We reminded each other that our self-doubts were probably imposter syndrome creeping in. I learned a lot from Alexandre and the other faculty at Antioch. It is quite remarkable to work and learn in an environment that is focused on supportive growth. It leads to quality work and innovative results.

As a leader, you likely experience imposter syndrome from time to time. So do your team members. While you cannot get in their heads and control their inner thoughts, you can provide encouragement and tell them when they are doing a good job. Tell them you are proud of them and that you value their work. Perhaps follow Alexandre's lead and talk about imposter syndrome as a team. Most importantly, do not let your inner critic, your self-doubt—whatever you want to call it—stop you from getting creative and serving those who matter with your innovations.

AS A LEADER, you want your team to have as few barriers to innovation as possible. Some barriers you may be able to eliminate for your team. Others will require a team effort to work through. What can you do to eliminate these barriers for your team? Or what can you all work on together?

Barriers to new ideas, new approaches, and new ways of doing things are normal. They are part of our human experience. The barriers are part of what makes innovation risky and challenging. They also make you stronger and more resilient, and they make innovative wins so much sweeter.

9

For Humanity

WENT TO AN AMAZING but unusual school for my PhD. There were no grades because grades decrease learning. There were no deadlines because we were adults and could set our own damn schedules. The expectation, the requirement, was that your work, your writing, and your research were about doing good in the world. At Antioch University we were gifted T-shirts with a quote from the founder, Horace Mann: "Be afraid to die until you have won some victory for humanity." I am not sure I will ever reach that aspiration, but I think about it frequently. It was top of mind on a warm June day sitting on an airplane in Atlanta.

Several years ago, I was invited to Mayo Clinic to lead a full-day creativity training for a group of their leaders. Given my mom's experience with Mayo (which you read about in chapter 1), it felt quite profound to have the privilege to work with them. I poured my heart into ensuring the program was top-notch, relevant, and meaningful to the twenty leaders I would be working with. I had been really nervous about teaching leaders at Mayo Clinic about deliberate creativity. Imposter syndrome reared its ugly head, and I started questioning why they wanted to learn from me. What did I have to offer to the best hospital in the world? There were more experienced creativity trainers and researchers than me. I wanted to do a really good job. I wanted to be good. I wanted to wow them! As the day arrived, I was getting more nervous. Then I had a big aha moment in an unexpected place.

I sat at the gate for my flight from Atlanta, Georgia, to Rochester, Minnesota, and heard the airline staff announce that it was time to board. At that moment, I realized I needed to use the bathroom, but I did not have time. It was a small plane and boarding would be quick, so I decided to just use the bathroom on the plane. (Yes, I was that person.) My seat was in row one, and as luck would have it, the only bathroom was in the back. I dropped my backpack in my seat and walked down the aisle. There were only a few other people on the plane, but I was blocked by an elderly couple who boarded early. They were leaning over their seats and rummaging through their things. I could not see what they were doing. After a minute or two, I said, "Is there anything I can help you with?"

The woman barked an order at the man. (This is how I knew they were married.) Then she turned to me and politely said, "I'm sorry. We'll be just another minute."

At that moment, I saw in her seat a box with a brown neo-prene case and clear tubing running up to her face. They had been trying to untangle her oxygen tank. I wanted to send her all the empathy and calming vibes I could. I put my hand on her shoulder and said, "There's no rush. Take your time."

A few minutes later they were settled, and I continued down the aisle. When I came out of the bathroom, the small plane was nearly full and the aisle was blocked with passengers stowing their luggage. As I watched, I saw several oxygen tanks being carried down the aisle and other contraptions I did not recognize. There were more medical devices on this

Innovation is
about changing
lives and
**doing good in
the world.**

flight than any flight I had ever been on! I realized at least half of these passengers were flying across the country to seek help from Mayo Clinic.

When I got to my seat, I thought about all the passengers. I thought about the couple I waited behind in the aisle. Before we boarded, there had been a woman in the gate area talking on the phone about her recent cancer diagnosis. Another young woman had a thirty-second seizure and a couple of people rushed over to help. When she came to, she laughed it off and said, "Well I'm good now. That's my one for the day!"

I felt the significance of my upcoming work with Mayo. I still felt nervous about the program the following day. Then suddenly, I felt a wash of gratitude and a surprising calmness rush over me. My eyes filled with tears. It hit me.

This was not about me. This was not about me being good or impressing anyone. This was not even about the twenty leaders who were going to spend a full day with me learning about creativity and innovation. This was about all the people on that flight. This was about the 1.3 million people Mayo serves each year. This was about the eight billion people on our planet who might benefit from a new procedure or practice invented at Mayo.

Innovation is not about us. It is not about the accolades or rewards or getting our name on the patent. It is about serving others. It is about changing lives and doing good in the world. When we focus too much on ourselves, our work is not as strong or impactful. When we focus on serving others, it leads us to profound results.

If you keep in mind who you are serving, it can keep you motivated and focused on innovation. You might not be in a field where the changes you make are the difference between life and death, but in some way, your work is about improving others' lives. Nearly all of what we create, design, and invent is about improving something for someone somewhere. Who are you serving? What do they need? What is a problem that you and your team are facing that you can solve through collaborative creativity? Creativity is about identifying problems and finding solutions and doing that over and over again. Now you know how to lead your team to be deliberate creatives. You know how to cultivate your team purpose, facilitate strong team dynamics, and lead the team creative process. Now comes the hard part.

It is easy to read a book. Despite what I said in chapter 1, reading this book will not change your team. It will not make your team more creative, except on one condition: You do the work. You work on building your skills to lead your team on this journey to be a Deliberate Creative Team.

Lead your team through the exercises in this book, share the concepts with them. Work together to learn to be more creative. Learning together builds team trust and cohesion, and you already know how important that is.

When your team gets clear on its purpose, builds strong team dynamics together, and everyone knows and uses the creative process, then creativity will flourish. That creativity will lead to innovative results so that you and your team can positively impact your clients, customers, communities, and even the world.

I am excited to see what your team creates, designs, and invents. We need your brilliance.

Acknowledgments

WRITING A BOOK is a weird, yet profound experience. It requires the juxtaposition of different activities. First, I needed quiet solo time, which included thinking, writing, editing, lots of Post-it Notes, scrap paper, dozens of drafts, and occasional chocolate. Then I also needed a community of people to push me, challenge me, give me hugs, laugh at the blunders, and cry with me when it got too hard. I could not have done it without all the support I received. I know because I tried for a long time, and the book just stayed stuck in my head.

I have wanted to write this book for years and finally AJ Harper, author of *Write a Must-Read*, came along and was the catalyst I needed. When I read her book, I knew AJ was the person I needed to bring the book out of my head and onto the page. Thank you, AJ, for your guidance, insights, support, and great conversations along the way. And to Laura Stone for your endless encouragement during writing sprints, and to the entire Top Three Community for being awesome humans.

The team at Page Two has been amazing. Thank you to Jesse Finkelstein for quickly saying yes and taking a chance on me. To Kendra Ward, my editor, for teaching me some important writing nuances, rearranging large chunks into a more coherent flow, and continually pushing me to make this book better. To Adrineh Der-Boghossian, Carmen Ho, Taysia Louie, Madelaine Manson, David Marsh, Crissy Boylan, and Tessa Eisenberg for your work in bringing this book to life.

The foundation of this book was the research I conducted as part of my dissertation at Antioch University. I am forever grateful to my committee of Mitchell Kusy, Carol Baron, and Susan Keller-Mathers for their countless hours of advice, instruction, edits, suggestions, and guidance to help me design and implement a strong study. Thank you to creativity expert James Kaufman, the external reader of my dissertation. All of you helped me shape a more valuable piece of research that continues to help teams be more creative.

Thank you to the hundreds of researchers and practitioners in creativity and leadership from whom I have learned. We all stand on the shoulders of giants, and it is only because of earlier work paving the way that I could write this book. I hope that something in here contributes to the collective canon of research on creativity in teams.

To my consulting clients, I am thrilled you want to be more creative and push innovation in your work. Your contributions to the world are making this planet better for all of us. Thank you.

Thank you to the early readers, Priscilla Gill, Nick Orlowski, Michael Kuscak, and Amy Whitney, for your insights and feedback. Thank you to those I interviewed for the book: Elizabeth Andre, Lyne Fontana, Joy Nelson, Jennifer Espinola, Tom Heck, Erika Kofler, Steph Monson Dahl, Stephanie Moore, Sarah Goldman, Walker Jones, Jay Roberts, Michael Ciannilli, and many others who engaged in conversations about creativity in your organizations.

Thank you to my parents, Ron Climer and Frances Demetree-Dasher, the rest of my big family, and the many friends who asked about the book along the way. Your encouragement helped me feel more connected and less alone.

Thank you to the staff and historians at Mayo Clinic who helped me find some elusive reference materials. Thank you to the doctors and staff at Mayo Clinic who saved my mom's life in 1973. Without you, I would not exist.

To my daughter, Tiff, I thought of you often as I wrote. Your dream to be a writer one day inspired me to keep going. It is hard work, but I know you have it in you. One day I will be reading the acknowledgments section of a book you wrote. I can't wait.

Thank you to my wife, Julie Koenke, for your continual encouragement and patience. There were moments when I was pushing hard to meet a deadline. I would apologize for the messy dining room table covered in notes and reference books, and you would say, "It's okay. It's part of the process," and gently kiss my head. Then head off to make us dinner. How did I get so lucky?

Notes

Introduction: You're Not Creative (or So You Were Told)

1 IBM, *Capitalizing on Complexity: Insights on the Global Chief Executive Officer Study* (IBM Institute for Business Value, 2010).

2 World Economic Forum, *Future of Jobs Report*, 2020, weforum.org/publications/the-future-of-jobs-report-2020.

3 Colette Martin and Kristi Hedges, "Creativity Is the New Black," *Forbes*, updated August 19, 2011, forbes.com/sites/work-in-progress/2010/07/16/creativity-is-the-new-black.

4 Temple Grandin, *Visual Thinking: The Hidden Gifts of People Who Think in Pictures, Patterns, and Abstractions* (New York: Riverhead Books, 2023).

Chapter 1: Why You Need to Innovate Now

1 Ellen Whelan and Matthew D. Dacy, *The Little Book of Mayo Clinic Values* (Rochester, MN: Mayo Foundation for Medical Education and Research, 2017), 4–6.

2 The story about Frances came from numerous in-person and phone conversations with Frances Demetree-Dasher, Ron Climer, and the author between 2018 and 2024, as well as Frances's Mayo Clinic medical records.

3 *A New Way of Seeing: The First CAT Scan at Mayo Clinic* (Mayo Clinic Heritage Films, 2023), film, 23 min., history.mayoclinic.org/books-films/heritage-films/a-new-way-of-seeing-the-first-cat-scan-at-mayo-clinic.

4 Whelan and Dacy, *The Little Book of Mayo Clinic Values*, 15.

5 Bruce Fye, *Caring for the Heart: Mayo Clinic and the Rise of Specialization* (New York: Oxford University Press, 2015), 13. By permission of Mayo Foundation for Medical Education and Research. Courtesy

of the W. Bruce Fye Center for the History of Medicine, Mayo Clinic, Rochester, Minnesota.

6 "1905: Frozen section technique revolutionizes surgery," Mayo Clinic Contributions to Medicine, 2022, history.mayoclinic.org/wp-content/uploads/2022/11/1905.pdf.

7 Jennifer O'Hara, "An Inside Look at Invention at Mayo Clinic," *Mayo Clinic Connect*, November 29, 2022, connect.mayoclinic.org/blog/podcasts/newsfeed-post/an-inside-look-at-invention-at-mayo-clinic; Mayo Clinic Department of Business Development, email to the author, May 1, 2024.

8 Sarah Pruitt, "When the Sears Catalog Sold Everything from Houses to Hubcaps," History.com, updated October 6, 2023, history.com/news/sears-catalog-houses-hubcaps.

9 Lucy Bayly, "Sears, Once the World's Biggest Retailer, Now Faces Bankruptcy," NBC News, October 10, 2018, nbcnews.com/business/business-news/125-year-old-sears-file-bankruptcy-report-n918446.

10 Sears Holdings, "Sears Holdings Reports Fourth Quarter and Full Year 2016 Results," archived from the original, March 9, 2017, web.archive.org/web/20170312042021/https://searsholdings.com/docs/investor/eap/q4-2016-shc-earnings-release.pdf.

11 Jay Roberts, provost of Warren Wilson College, in conversation with the author, January 29, 2024, video.

12 Northland College, "Northland College Seeks $12 million to Avoid Closure, Reimagine Its Future," March 11, 2024, northland.edu/news/northland-college-seeks-12-million-to-avoid-closure-reimagine-its-future.

13 Elizabeth Andre, professor of outdoor education, Northland College, in conversation with the author, June 5, 2024, video.

14 Sarah Goldman, community programs director, North Carolina Outward Bound School, in conversation with the author, January 31, 2024, video.

15 Jan Letendre, chief financial officer, North Carolina Outward Bound School, in conversation with the author, July 3, 2024, phone.

16 Jonathan A. Plucker, Ronald A. Beghetto, and Gayle T. Dow, "Why Isn't Creativity More Important to Educational Psychologists? Potentials, Pitfalls, and Future Directions in Creativity Research," *Educational Psychologist* 39 (2004): 83–96, doi.org/10.1207/s15326985ep3902_1.

17 Anahita Baregheh, Jennifer Rowley, and Sally Sambrook, "Towards a
    Multidisciplinary Definition of Innovation," *Management Decision* 47,
    no. 8 (2009), 1323-39, doi.org/10.1108/00251740910984578.
18 Pamela Tierney and Steven M. Farmer, "Creative Self-Efficacy
    Development and Creative Performance Over Time," *Journal of
    Applied Psychology* 96 (2011), 277-93, doi.org/10.1037/a0020952.

Chapter 2: Not by Magic or Chance

1   Diane F. Baker and Susan I. Baker, "To 'Catch the Sparkling Glow':
    A Canvas for Creativity in the Management Classroom," *Academy
    of Management Learning & Education* 11, no. 4 (2012): 704-21,
    doi.org/10.5465/amle.2010.0003.
2   Robert Epstein, Steven Schmidt, and Regina Warfel, "Measuring
    and Training Creativity Competencies: Validation of a New Test,"
    Creativity Research Journal 20, no. 1 (2008): 7-12, doi.org/10.1080/
    10400410701839876; Gerard J. Puccio, Roger L. Firestien, Christina
    Coyle, and Cristina Masucci, "A Review of the Effectiveness of CPS
    Training: A Focus on Workplace Issues," *Creativity and Innovation
    Management* 15, no. 1 (2006): 19-33; Ginamarie Scott, Lyle E. Leritz,
    and Michael D. Mumford, "Types of Creativity Training: Approaches
    and Their Effectiveness," *Creativity Research Journal* 16, no. 4 (2004):
    361-88; Robert J. Sternberg, "Teaching for Creativity," in *Nurturing
    Creativity in the Classroom*, Ronald A. Beghetto and James C. Kaufman,
    eds. (New York: Cambridge University Press, 2010), 394-414; E. Paul
    Torrance, "Can We Teach Children to Think Creatively?" *Journal
    of Creative Behavior* 6, no. 2 (1972): 114-43, doi.org/10.1002/j.2162
    -6057.1972.tb00923.x.
3   Tom Wujec, "Build a Tower, Build a Team," TED Talk, 2010, ted.com/
    talks/tom_wujec_build_a_tower_build_a_team.
4   Puccio, Firestien, Coyle, and Masucci, "A Review of the Effectiveness
    of CPS Training"; Hsen-Hsing Ma, "A Synthetic Analysis of the
    Effectiveness of Single Components and Packages in Creativity
    Training Programs," *Creativity Research Journal* 18, no. 4 (2006):
    435-46, doi.org/10.1207/s15326934crj1804_3; Ginamarie Scott,
    Lyle E. Leritz, and Michael D. Mumford, "The Effectiveness of
    Creativity Training: A Quantitative Review," *Creativity Research
    Journal* 16, no. 4 (2004): 361-88, doi.org/10.1080/104004
    10409534549.

5 Puccio, Firestien, Coyle, and Masucci, "A Review of the Effectiveness of CPS Training."

6 Roger L. Firestien, *Leading on the Creative Edge: Gaining Competitive Advantage through the Power of Creative Problem Solving* (Colorado Springs: Pinon Press, 1996), 85–87.

7 Epstein, Schmidt, and Warfel, "Measuring and Training Creativity Competencies."

8 Tom Heck, in conversation with the author, March 1, 2023, video.

9 Ute Hülsheger, Neil Anderson, and Jesus Salgado, "Team-Level Predictors of Innovation at Work: A Comprehensive Meta-Analysis Spanning Three Decades of Research," *Journal of Applied Psychology* 94, no. 5 (2009): 1128–45, doi.org/10.1037/a0015978.

10 Hülsheger, Anderson, and Salgado, "Team-Level Predictors of Innovation at Work"; Simon Taggar, "Individual Creativity and Group Ability to Utilize Individual Creative Resources: A Multilevel Model," *Academy of Management Journal* 45, no. 2 (2002): 315–30, doi.org/10.2307/3069349.

11 Amy Climer, "The Development of the Creative Synergy Scale" (PhD diss., Antioch University, 2016), aura.antioch.edu/etds/270. The scale was originally called the Creative Synergy Scale, but the name was later changed to the Deliberate Creative Team Scale.

12 Jon R. Katzenbach and Douglas K. Smith, *The Wisdom of Teams: Creating the High Performance Organization* (New York: HarperBusiness, 1999), 43–64; James Kouzes and Barry Posner, *The Leadership Challenge: How to Keep Getting Extraordinary Things Done in Organizations* (San Francisco: Jossey-Bass, 1995), 116–25; Carl Larson and Frank LaFasto, *Teamwork: What Must Go Right / What Can Go Wrong* (Newbury Park, CA: Sage Publications, 1989).

13 Linda A. Hill, Greg Brandeau, Emily Truelove, and Kent Lineback, *Collective Genius: The Art and Practice of Leading Innovation* (Boston: Harvard Business Review Press, 2014); Robert Sutton and Andrew Hargadon, "Brainstorming Groups in Context: Effectiveness in a Product Design Firm," *Administrative Science Quarterly* 41 (1996): 685–718.

14 R. Keith Sawyer, *Explaining Creativity: The Science of Human Innovation*, 2nd edition (New York: Oxford University Press, 2012), 243–46.

15 For examples, see Robert Garmston and Bruce Wellman, *The Adaptive School: A Sourcebook for Developing Collaborative Groups* (Norwood,

MA: Christopher-Gordon, 2009) and Scott G. Isaksen, K. Brian Dorval, and Donald J. Treffinger, *Creative Approaches to Problem Solving: A Framework for Innovation and Change*, 3rd edition (Thousand Oaks, CA: Sage Publications, 2011).

Chapter 3: The Source of Innovation in Organizations

1 Jon R. Katzenbach and Douglas K. Smith, *The Wisdom of Teams: Creating the High Performance Organization* (New York: HarperBusiness, 1999), 15–19.

2 Tom Kelley, *The Art of Innovation: Lessons in Creativity from IDEO, America's Leading Design Firm* (New York: Doubleday, 2001); Paul B. Paulus and Bernard A. Nijstad, *Group Creativity: Innovation through Collaboration* (New York: Oxford University Press, 2003); Keith Sawyer, *Group Genius: The Creative Power of Collaboration* (New York: Basic Books, 2007); Chiayu Tu, "A Multilevel Investigation of Factors Influencing Creativity in NPD Teams," *Industrial Marketing Management* 38, no. 1 (2009): 119–26, doi.org/10.1016/j.indmarman .2007.10.001; Ute Hülsheger, Neil Anderson, and Jesus Salgado, "Team-Level Predictors of Innovation at Work: A Comprehensive Meta-Analysis Spanning Three Decades of Research," *Journal of Applied Psychology* 94, no. 5 (2009): 1128–45, doi.org/10.1037/ a0015978.

3 Stefan Wuchty, Benjamin F. Jones, and Brian Uzzi, "The Increasing Dominance of Teams in Production of Knowledge," *Science* 316, no. 5827 (2007): 1036–39, doi.org/10.1126/science.1136099; Jonathon N. Cummings and Sara Kiesler, "Collaborative Research across Disciplinary and Organizational Boundaries," *Social Studies of Science* 35, no. 5 (2005): 703–722, doi.org/10.1177/030631270505553.

4 Mihalyi Csikszentmihalyi, *Creativity: Flow and the Psychology of Discovery and Invention* (New York: HarperCollins, 1996), 12–16.

5 Rita Bissola and Barbara Imperatori, "Organizing Individual and Collective Creativity: Flying in the Face of Creativity Clichés," *Creativity and Innovation Management* 20, no. 2 (2011): 77–89, doi.org/10.1111/j.1467-8691.2011.00597.x.

6 Katzenbach and Smith, *The Wisdom of Teams*, 45.

7 Katzenbach and Smith, *The Wisdom of Teams*, 91.

8 Brittany App, *Where There Once Was Water: A Song for the Sacred in All of Us* (2021), film, 74 min.

Chapter 4: The Clarifying Force of Team Purpose

1 Jeffrey K. Pinto and John E. Prescott, "Changes in Critical Success Factor Importance over the Life of a Project," *Academy of Management Proceedings* 1 (1987): 328-32, doi.org/10.5465/ambpp.1987.17534396.

2 Craig L. Pearce and Michael D. Ensley, "A Reciprocal and Longitudinal Investigation of the Innovation Process: The Central Role of Shared Vision in Product and Process Innovation Teams (PPITs)," *Journal of Organizational Behavior* 25 (2004): 259-78, doi.org/10.1(X)2/job.235.

3 Ana Cristina Costa and Neil Anderson, "Measuring Trust in Teams: Development and Validation of a Multifaceted Measure of Formative and Reflective Indicators of Team Trust," *European Journal of Work and Organizational Psychology* 20, no. 1 (2011): 119-54, doi.org/10.1080/13594320903272083.

4 James W. Bishop and K. Dow Scott, "An Examination of Organizational and Team Commitment in a Self-Directed Team Environment," *Journal of Applied Psychology* 85, no. 3 (2000): 439-50, doi.org/10.1037/0021-9010.85.3.439.

5 Ed Catmull and Amy Wallace, *Creativity, Inc.: Overcoming the Unforeseen Forces That Stand in the Way of True Inspiration* (New York: Random House, 2014), 73.

6 Catmull and Wallace, *Creativity, Inc.*, 74.

7 Carl Larson and Frank LaFasto, *Teamwork: What Must Go Right / What Can Go Wrong* (Newbury Park, CA: Sage Publications, 1989), 13-38.

8 Johnathan R. Cromwell, "Dynamic Problem Solving for Breakthrough Innovation: The Case of a Social Robot" (PhD diss., Harvard Business School, 2018), 88.

Chapter 5: The Key Ingredients in Team Dynamics

1 Jim Harter, "Is Quiet Quitting Real?" Workplace for Gallup, September 6, 2022, gallup.com/workplace/398306/quiet-quitting -real.aspx; Anthony C. Klotz and Mark C. Bolino, "When Quiet Quitting Is Worse Than the Real Thing," *Harvard Business Review*, September 15, 2022, hbr.org/2022/09/when-quiet-quitting-is -worse-than-the-real-thing.

2 Amy C. Edmondson, *The Fearless Organization: Creating Psychological Safety in the Workplace for Learning, Innovation, and Growth* (New York: John Wiley & Sons, 2018); Amy Edmondson, "Psychological Safety and Learning Behavior in Work Teams," *Administrative Science Quarterly* 44 (1999): 350-83, doi.org/10.2307/2666999.

3 Gloria Barczak, Felicia Lassk, and Jay Mulki, "Antecedents of Team Creativity: An Examination of Team Emotional Intelligence, Team Trust and Collaborative Culture," *Creativity and Innovation Management* 19, no. 4 (2010): 332–45, doi.org/10.1111/j.1467 -8691.2010.00574.x.

4 Charles Duhigg, "What Google Learned from Its Quest to Build the Perfect Team," *The New York Times Magazine*, February 25, 2016, nytimes.com/2016/02/28/magazine/what-google-learned-from -its-quest-to-build-the-perfect-team.html.

5 Karen Jehn, "A Multimethod Examination of the Benefits and Detriments of Intragroup Conflict," *Administrative Science Quarterly* 40 (1995): 256–82, doi.org/10.2307/2393638.

6 *Investigation of the Challenger Accident (Volume 1): Hearings Before the Committee on Science and Technology*, House of Representatives, Ninety-ninth Congress, Second Session, No. 137, 1986.

7 Glen Whyte, "Recasting Janis's Groupthink Model: The Key Role of Collective Efficacy in Decision Fiascoes," *Organizational Behavior and Human Decision Processes* 73, no. 2/3 (1998): 185–209, doi.org/ 10.1006/obhd.1998.2761.

8 Irving Janis, "Groupthink," in *A First Look at Communication Theory*, Em Griffin, ed. (New York: McGraw Hill, 1991), 235–46.

9 Michael Ciannilli, manager of the *Apollo, Challenger, Columbia* Lessons Learned Program, NASA, in conversation with the author, February 29, 2024, video.

10 Jerry Hirshberg, *The Creative Priority: Driving Innovative Business in the Real World* (New York: HarperCollins, 1998), chapter 1, Kindle.

11 Hirshberg, *The Creative Priority*, chapter 1.

12 Linda A. Hill, Greg Brandeau, Emily Truelove, and Kent Lineback, *Collective Genius: The Art and Practice of Leading Innovation* (Boston: Harvard Business Review Press, 2014), 138.

13 Viktoria Stray and Nils Brede Moe, "Understanding Coordination in Global Software Engineering: A Mixed-Methods Study on the Use of Meetings and Slack," *Journal of Systems and Software* 170 (2020): 110717; Rachel Emma Silverman, "Where's the Boss? Trapped in a Meeting," *Wall Street Journal*, February 14, 2012, wsj.com/articles/ SB10001424052970204642604577215013504567548.

14 Alex "Sandy" Pentland, "The New Science of Building Great Teams," *Harvard Business Review*, April 2012, hbr.org/2012/04/the-new -science-of-building-great-teams.

15 Ute Hülsheger, Neil Anderson, and Jesus Salgado, "Team-Level Predictors of Innovation at Work: A Comprehensive Meta-Analysis Spanning Three Decades of Research," *Journal of Applied Psychology* 94, no. 5 (2009): 1128–45, doi.org/10.1037/a0015978.

16 Jan Kratzer, Roger Th. A.J. Leenders, and Jo M.L. van Engelen, "Stimulating the Potential: Creative Performance and Communication in Innovation Teams," *Creativity and Innovation Management* 13, no. 1 (March 2004): 63–71, doi.org/10.1111/j.1467-8691.2004.00294.x.

Chapter 6: The Transformative Power of Team Creative Process

1 Robert J. Garmston and Bruce M. Wellman, *The Adaptive School: A Sourcebook for Developing Collaborative Groups* (Norwood, MA: Christopher-Gordon, 2009); Scott G. Isaksen, K. Brian Dorval, and Donald J. Treffinger, *Creative Approaches to Problem Solving: A Framework for Innovation and Change*, 3rd edition (Thousand Oaks, CA: Sage Publications, 2011), 9–51.

2 Arthur Cropley, "In Praise of Convergent Thinking," *Creativity Research Journal* 18 (2006): 391–404, doi.org/10.1207/s15326934crj1803_13.

3 This creative problem solving model has evolved over several decades and is based on the work of Alex F. Osborn, *Applied Imagination: Principles and Procedures of Creative Problem Solving* (New York: Scribner's, 1953); Sidney J. Parnes, Ruth B. Noller, and Angelo M. Biondi, *Guide to Creative Action: Revised Edition of Creative Behavior Guidebook* (New York: Scribner's, 1977); Blair Miller, Roger Firestien, Jonathan Vehar, Plain Language Creative Problem-Solving Model, 1997; Gerard J. Puccio, Marie Mance, Mary C. Murdock, *Creative Leadership: Skills That Drive Change*, 2nd edition (Thousand Oaks, CA: Sage Publications, 2010); Blair Miller, Jonathan Vehar, Roger Firestien, Sarah Thurber, Dorte Nielsen, *Creativity Unbound: An Introduction to Creative Process*, 5th edition (Evanston, IL: FourSight Group LLC, 2011).

4 Gerard Puccio, "Creative Problem Solving Preferences: Their Identification and Implications," *Creativity and Innovation Management* 8, no. 3 (1999): 171–78, doi.org/10.1111/1467-8691 .00134; Sarah Thurber and Blair Miller, *Good Team, Bad Team: Lead Your People to Go After Big Challenges, Not Each Other* (Vancouver: Page Two, 2024).

5 Roger L. Firestien, *Solve the Real Problem: Because What You Think Is the Problem Is Usually Not the Problem* (Green Tractor Publishing, 2024).

6   Alex Osborn, *Your Creative Power: How to Use Imagination* (New York: Dell, 1948), 285.

7   Brian Mullen, Craig Johnson, and Eduardo Salas, "Productivity Loss in Brainstorming Groups: A Meta-Analytic Integration," *Basic and Applied Social Psychology* 12, no. 1 (1991): 2-23, doi.org/ 10.1207/s15324834basp1201_1; Tudor Rickards and Brian L. Freedman, "Procedures for Managers in Idea-Deficient Situations: An Examination of Brainstorming Approaches," *Journal of Management Studies* 15, no. 1 (1978): 43-55, doi.org/10.1111/j.1467-6486.1978 .tb00908.x; Donald W. Taylor, Paul C. Berry, and Clifford H. Block, "Does Group Participation When Using Brainstorming Facilitate or Inhibit Creative Thinking?" *Administrative Science Quarterly* 3, no. 1 (1958): 23-47, doi.org/10.2307/2390603.

8   Taylor, Berry, and Block, "Does Group Participation When Using Brainstorming Facilitate or Inhibit Creative Thinking?"

9   Rickards and Freedman, "Procedures for Managers in Idea-Deficient Situations."

10 Robert Sutton and Andrew Hargadon, "Brainstorming Groups in Context: Effectiveness in a Product Design Firm," *Administrative Science Quarterly* 41, no. 4 (1996): 685-718, doi.org/10.2307/ 2393872.

11 Scott Isaksen and John Gaulin, "A Reexamination of Brainstorming Research: Implications for Research and Practice," *Gifted Child Quarterly* 49, no. 4 (2005): 315-29, doi.org/10.1177/ 001698620504900405.

12 Amy Climer and Dani Chesson, "Episode 91: The Skills You Need to Be a Design Thinker," April 5, 2018, in *The Deliberate Creative*, podcast, climerconsulting.com/091.

13 PPCO (pluses, potentials, concerns, overcoming concerns) was invented by Diane Foucar-Szocki, Bill Shepard, and Roger Firestien in 1982.

Chapter 7: From Creative Inspiration to Innovative Integration

1   Mihalyi Csikszentmihalyi, *Creativity: Flow and the Psychology of Discovery and Invention* (New York: HarperCollins, 1996), 27-45.

2   You can learn more about FourSight's work at foursightonline.com.

3   Joy Nelson, information technology consultant, in conversation with the author, February 17, 2023, video.

4   Daniel Pink, *Drive: The Surprising Truth about What Motivates Us* (New York: Riverhead Books, 2011), 49.

5 James Burroughs, Darren W. Dahl, C. Page Moreau, Amitava Chattopadhyay, and Gerald J. Gorn, "Facilitating and Rewarding Creativity during New Product Development," *Journal of Marketing* 74, no. 4 (2011): 53–67, doi.org/10.1509/jmkg.75.4.53.

6 Teresa Amabile and Steven Kramer, *The Progress Principle: Using Small Wins to Ignite Joy, Engagement, and Creativity at Work* (Massachusetts: Harvard Business Review Press, 2011), 18.

Chapter 8: How to Clear the Path for Creativity

1 ALS Association, "The ALS Ice Bucket Challenge: 10th Anniversary," accessed June 19, 2024, als.org/IBC.

2 Tom Kelley, *The Art of Innovation: Lessons in Creativity from IDEO, America's Leading Design Firm* (New York: Doubleday, 2001), 58.

3 Alfredo Muñoz Adánez, "Does Quantity Generate Quality? Testing the Fundamental Principle of Brainstorming," *Spanish Journal of Psychology* 8, no. 2 (2005): 215–20, doi.org/10.1017/S1138741600 005096; Paul B. Paulus, Nicholas W. Kohn, and Lauren E. Arditti, "Effects of Quantity and Quality Instructions on Brainstorming," *Journal of Creative Behavior* 45 (2011): 38–46, doi.org/10.1002/ J.2162-6057.2011.TB01083.X.

4 Daniel Coyle, *The Culture Code: The Secrets of Highly Successful Groups* (New York: Bantam Books, 2018), 219–26.

5 Ronald Heifetz, Alexander Grashow, and Marty Linsky, *The Practice of Adaptive Leadership: Tools and Tactics for Changing Your Organization and the World* (Massachusetts: Harvard Business Press, 2009), 19, 68.

6 David Rock, "SCARF: A Brain-Based Model for Collaborating with and Influencing Others," *NeuroLeadership Journal* 1 (2008): 1–9.

7 Mihalyi Csikszentmihalyi, distinguished professor of psychology and management at Claremont Graduate University, interview with the author, December 21, 2011, phone.

8 Mihalyi Csikszentmihalyi, *Creativity: Flow and the Psychology of Discovery and Invention* (New York: HarperCollins, 1996), 65.

9 Jennifer Wilson, *Waking Up to Your Worth: Ten Touchstones for Overcoming Imposter Syndrome* (self-pub., Motivational M.D., 2020), xix.

10 "The One Question Oprah Winfrey Says Every Guest Asked," Bloomberg Originals, March 1, 2017, youtube.com/watch?v= 343kpgulUXU.

PHOTO: ERICA MUELLER

About the Author

D R. AMY CLIMER is a thought leader and consultant in innovation and team development. She teaches forward-thinking organizations how to unlock the creative potential in individuals and teams so they can innovate anytime. As the founder of Climer Consulting, she has significantly impacted for-profit and nonprofit organizations, government agencies, and universities. Her clients have included Mayo Clinic, the US Department of Homeland Security, FOX Sports, and the University of Wisconsin.

Dr. Climer holds a PhD in leadership and change from Antioch University. Her research led to the Deliberate Creative Team Scale, designed to measure the three critical factors of team creativity. Her TEDx Talk, "The Power of Deliberate Creative Teams," explains her research and philosophies on innovation.

As a keynote speaker and emcee, Dr. Climer was recognized as a Certified Speaking Professional by the National Speakers Association. She is also trained in creative problem solving, the FourSight Thinking System, and Immunity to Change.

She is the designer of Climer Cards, a creativity and team-building tool used by thousands of facilitators and trainers to deepen conversations and generate ideas. Dr. Climer's relentless pursuit of creativity and leadership excellence was recognized in 2016 when she received the Karl Rohnke Creativity Award from the Association for Experiential Education.

In addition to her professional work, Dr. Climer leads whitewater canoeing courses for the North Carolina Outward Bound School. When not working, she can be found building something in her woodshop or paddling on a river. Amy lives with her wife in Asheville, North Carolina.

Deliberate Creative Teams

Thank you! I am honored and excited that you have read this book and are on your way to leading a Deliberate Creative Team. But the book is just the beginning. I have additional resources to help you, your team, and your entire organization reach your creative potential.

Free extras: Visit climerconsulting.com/extras for the free tools and templates mentioned throughout the book as well as additional resources for leading Deliberate Creative Teams.

Customized support: If you would like to book me to keynote or emcee your event, lead a training for your team, or set up individual coaching, you can learn more by reaching out to me at climerconsulting.com.

Climer Cards: To order Climer Cards or join a free workshop, visit climercards.com.

Bulk purchases: If you want to share this book with your organization or colleagues, visit climerconsulting.com/book.

Let's connect on social at:

- linkedin.com/in/amyclimer
- instagram.com/amyclimer and instagram.com/climercards
- facebook.com/climerconsulting
- youtube.com/amyclimer

www.ingramcontent.com/pod-product-compliance
Lightning Source LLC
Chambersburg PA
CBHW030508210326
41597CB00013B/837

9 7 8 1 7 7 4 5 8 4 9 3 4